CONNECTICUT COAST

To my father and mother, Lou and Sarah Ross

With love and fond memories of many drives to the rocks and the Stone House in Guilford

CONNECTICUT COAST

A Town-by-Town Illustrated History

DIANA ROSS McCAIN

Photographs from
The Connecticut Historical Society

Guilford, Connecticut

Project Manager: Jessica Haberman
Layout: Joanna Beyer
Text design: Libby Kingsbury and Sheryl P. Kober
Maps courtesy of the Connecticut Historical Society
Jackie Kennedy photo p. 242 by U.S. Navy

Library of Congress Cataloging-in-Publication Data
McCain, Diana Ross.
  Connecticut coast : A town-by-town illustrated history / Diana Ross McCain ; images by the Connecticut Historical Society.
    p. cm.
  Includes bibliographical references.
  ISBN 978-0-7627-4723-8
  1. Atlantic Coast (Conn.)—History. 2. Atlantic Coast (Conn.)—History—Pictorial works. 3. Connecticut—History, Local.
4. Connecticut—History, Local—Pictorial works. I. Connecticut Historical Society. II. Title.
  F102.A85M38 2009
  974.6—dc22

                                                                                            2008036951

Printed in the United States of America

10 9 8 7 6 5 4 3 2 1

CONTENTS

ACKNOWLEDGMENTS

Connecticut Historical Society curator of graphics Nancy Finlay was an invaluable and congenial collaborator on assembling the illustrations for *Connecticut Coast.* Beyond making requested research materials available promptly and pleasantly, Nancy applied her extensive knowledge of CHS's holdings to turn up some of the most striking images in the book. CHS research center assistant Sierra Dixon ably performed the formidable task of scanning the lion's share of illustrations reproduced here.

Thanks are also due to Globe Pequot Press managing editor Amy Paradysz, who developed the concept of a book of images enriched by historical context that would embrace all the towns along the Connecticut coast into a project that has resulted in a publication unlike any other. Amy's energy, enthusiasm, coordination—and patience—made creating *Connecticut Coast* feasible and rewarding. I am also grateful to Globe Pequot Press assistant project manager Jess Haberman for assuming responsibility for the *Connecticut Coast* project in mid-process and seeing it through to completion with skill and professionalism.

I would also like to highlight the unique contribution of one particular individual to the book's contents. More than two dozen images in *Connecticut Coast* are drawings by John Warner Barber, which were reproduced as engravings in his pioneering book *Connecticut Historical Collections,* published in 1836. Anyone with an interest in Connecticut history owes a great debt to Barber. He created a visual record of Connecticut that, unbeknownst to him, would soon in large part be swept away in the wake of the industrial and transportation revolutions. Barber's drawings also are the earliest depictions of many Connecticut towns.

INTRODUCTION

Connecticut Coast serves up a surf-and-turf sampling of history from the two dozen Connecticut towns that border Long Island Sound by highlighting events that occurred both within and well beyond the sight and smell of salt water. Its stories and images were selected to represent aspects both transformative and trifling from the more than 370 years since the first Europeans arrived on the coast, from assembly lines to roller coasters, from circus elephants to "fat cat" entrepreneurs, from gory battlefields to serene town greens.

 Connecticut Coast seeks to spark in readers a kaleidoscope of emotions: amazement that the course of events transformed some shoreline towns into massive urban centers, while touching others with such a light hand that they look little different from what they did a century or more ago; astonishment at the hundreds of large factories that once proliferated in coastal towns, manufacturing everything from silk to padlocks; surprise that steamboats that would have been at home on Mark Twain's Mississippi River regularly plied the waters of Long Island Sound; horror at the barbarities human beings could inflict upon one another in time of war or at the devastation a single storm could wreak upon an unsuspecting population in a few short hours; nostalgia for good times at long-gone but fondly remembered spots like Savin Rock Amusement Park or the Griswold Hotel; and, most important of all, curiosity that will lead to further exploration of the vast, varied, and unique heritage of the Connecticut coast.

The Connecticut coastline, 1813, DETAIL

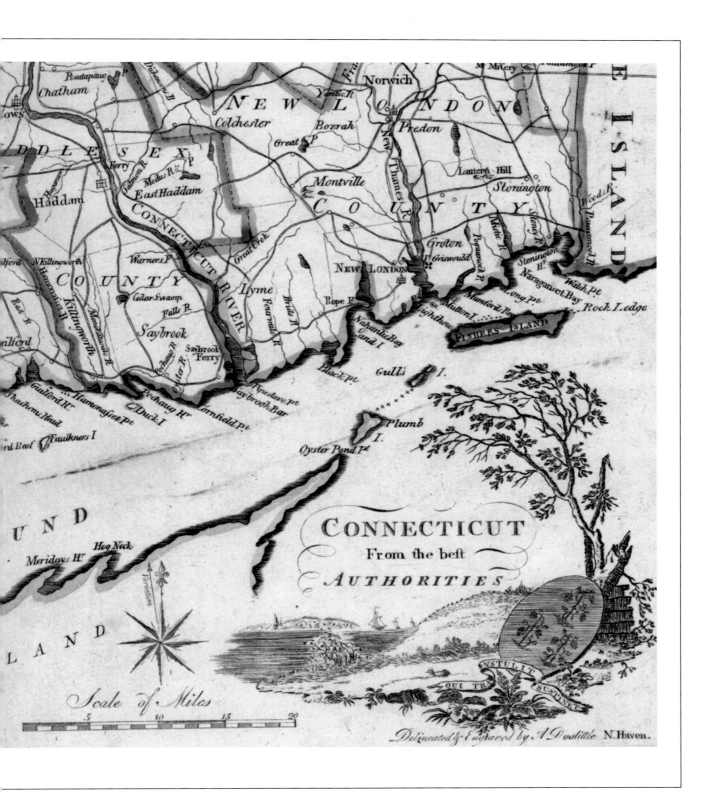

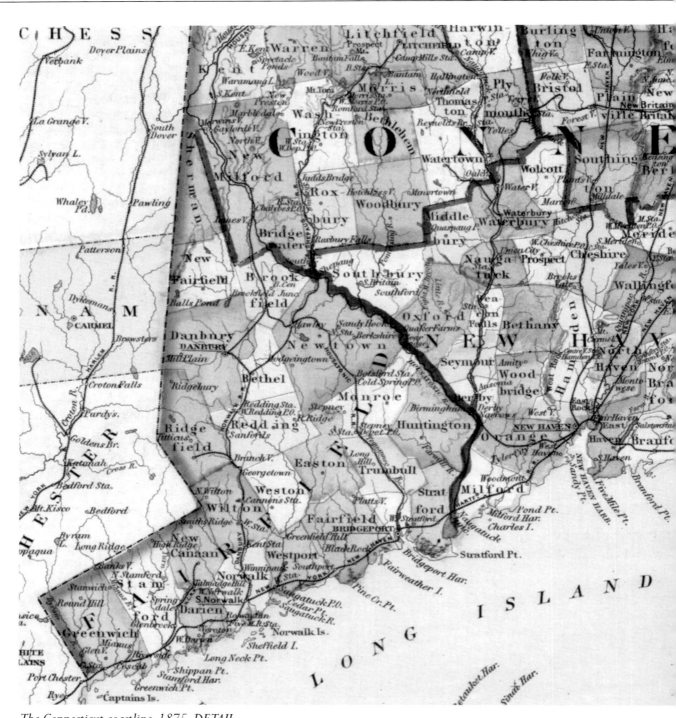

The Connecticut coastline, 1875, DETAIL

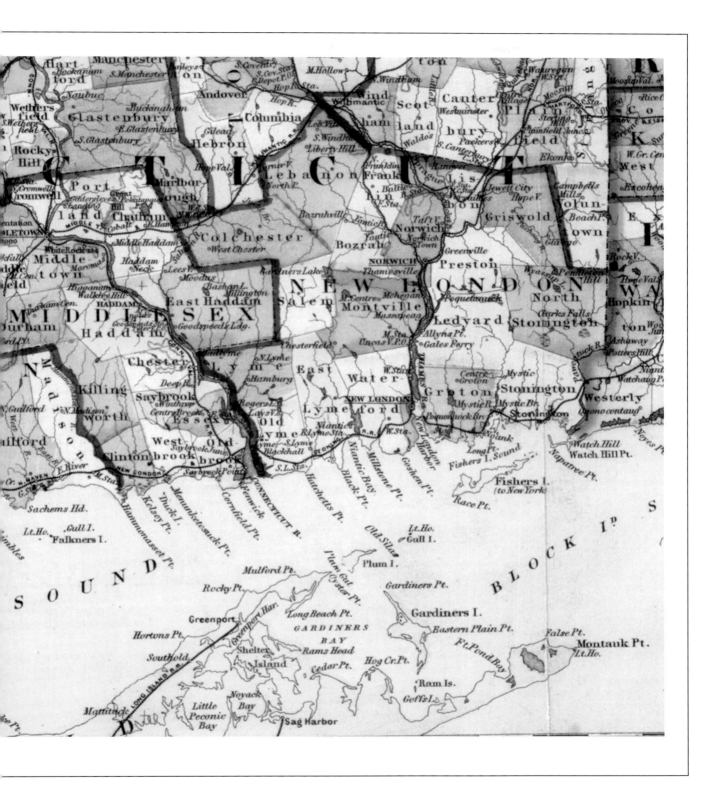

GREENWICH

*L*ocation, location, location. That real estate rule of thumb has influenced Greenwich's history, for good and ill, since its settlement in 1640. The aspect of Greenwich's location with the greatest impact has been its proximity to New York, particularly Manhattan, roughly twenty miles away as the crow flies.

Greenwich was purchased by private individuals technically acting under the auspices of the New Haven Colony, an independent governmental entity, in 1640. However, in 1642 Greenwich residents, not confident they could rely on the New Haven Colony to defend what was a remote frontier settlement against attack by Native Americans, put themselves under the jurisdiction of the Dutch settlement at New Amsterdam, modern New York City.

In 1650 the New Amsterdam and New Haven colonies reached an agreement that made Greenwich once again part of the New Haven Colony. Greenwich's residents, however, didn't formally acknowledge that change in authority until 1656—at which time Greenwich was made part of Stamford. At last, in 1665, Greenwich was incorporated as a separate town.

Subsequent generations of southwestern Connecticut residents forged strong commercial and social ties with New York, which tended to be broader minded about religious diversity and more conservative politically than Connecticut. In part because of this New York influence, when the American Revolution erupted in 1775, southwestern Connecticut counted more Loyalists—individuals who sympathized with the Crown in the war for independence—among its residents than other parts of the colony.

In Greenwich neighborhoods, friends, and even families were split bitterly over which side to support in the Revolution. Some Loyalists left—or were driven out—most never to return. Their property was confiscated by the State of Connecticut.

GEN. ISRAEL PUTNAM.

Gen. Israel Putnam, 1845–1846

Tradition says that in February of 1779 patriot Gen. Israel Putnam escaped a British raiding party in hot pursuit by plunging his horse down a stretch of seventy-four stone steps in West Greenwich so treacherously steep that the enemy lacked the nerve to follow him. Those steps, on what soon became known as Putnam's Hill, had almost completely disappeared by the 1830s. In 1900 a monument was placed at the spot where Putnam reportedly began his dangerous descent, and two years later twenty or so steps were cut into the hillside to represent the ones down which Putnam had daringly directed his horse. Gen. Putnam's ride is depicted on the Greenwich town seal.

From the late summer of 1776 until the end of the Revolution in 1783, the British controlled Manhattan and Long Island. Many Loyalists took refuge there, even signing up to bear arms on behalf of the king against the rebellious colonists.

Greenwich, separated by barely seven miles of water from Long Island, was a frequent target of enemy raids. The worst occurred in February of 1779, when a large force of British soldiers and Loyalists ransacked the town, leaving many families, according to a newspaper, "stript of everything but the clothes they had on."

Horse Show Day at Belle Haven, 1906

The Belle Haven Club was founded in 1889 and the very next year inaugurated its horse show. Depicted here in 1906, the cream of Greenwich society turned out to observe steeds in activities such as jumping over fences.

The horse show at the Belle Haven Club was soon just a memory, the victim of a financial downturn in 1907 that consisted of two crashes in the stock market, which lost half its value. Belle Haven, however, remains one of Greenwich's most exclusive private country clubs.

The arrival of the railroad in 1848 meant Greenwich's location, the source of much suffering during the Revolution, became the enormous advantage it has been ever since. Now just a short train ride from New York, Greenwich, still largely a farming town, attracted all manner of urbanites.

Among the first outsiders to appreciate Greenwich's special qualities were artists of the American Impressionism school, who took as their subject the gentle beauty of the countryside and coast. Greenwich's fields, historic houses, and shoreline were perfect subject matter for the Impressionists, who began coming as early as 1870.

The hub of what constituted a major artists' colony from the 1880s into the early 1900s was the fourteen-room boardinghouse in the Cos Cob section of Greenwich run

Clyde Fitch and Viola Allen in 1905
Locomobile Type E, ca. 1905

In this photograph, pioneering American play-wright Clyde Fitch and actress Viola Allen, who starred in two of Fitch's works on Broadway, get ready for a drive at Allen's country home in Greenwich. The automobile is a 1905 Loco-mobile Type E, manufactured in Bridgeport, Connecticut.

Fitch, who also had a home in Greenwich called Quiet Corner, enjoyed an astoundingly successful career writing for the stage. During his heyday he wrote more than sixty plays, including comedies and dramas. At one point, five of Fitch's plays were running on Broadway at the same time.

Fitch's career—and life—were cut tragically short not long after this photograph was taken. He died in France in 1909, of complications from emergency surgery performed after other treatments failed to relieve his chronic appendicitis. He was just forty-four.

Viola Allen starred in Fitch's 1905 Broadway play Talented Town, *which may explain why the two were motoring around Greenwich together that same year. She last performed in 1918 and died in 1948.*

HAND-COLORED.

View of Long Island Sound from Field Point Road, ca. 1910–1929

Long Island Sound lies in the distance in this photograph of the view from Field Point Road in the Belle Haven section, taken sometime around the turn of the twentieth century. Several of the homes to the left were still standing in the late twentieth century along a Field Point Road that had also been paved.

Pickwick Arms hotel, ca. 1940s

"New England's most beautiful family and transient hotel" was the boast made by the Pickwick Arms hotel, built in 1920. The Pickwick Arms on West Putnam Avenue was a landmark in Greenwich into the 1970s. It was razed to make way for a multibuilding office complex, Pickwick Plaza.

by the Holley family. Renowned American Impressionists like John Henry Twachtman, J. Alden Weir, and Childe Hassam spent summers in Greenwich in and around the Holley house, fanning out during the day to paint local scenes in the open air.

At Cos Cob, particularly in the casual, homey atmosphere of the Holley boardinghouse, the American Impressionists enjoyed the support and encouragement of fellow artists. Other creative personalities, such as novelists, journalists, and performing artists, were discovering Greenwich as well and often visited the Holley house. Journalist Lincoln Steffens and novelist Willa Cather were among the literati who frequented the Holley house. Today, the Bush-Holley House, the name derived by combining the names of the original builder and the Holleys, is one of a complex of buildings that serves as home to the Historical Society of the Town of Greenwich.

In the latter half of the nineteenth century, wealthy New Yorkers began to build summer homes in Greenwich or vacation at elegant resort hotels that sprang up. Newly minted millionaires who had made their fortunes in the industrial boom following the Civil War, or in some cases their children, built lavish mansions in Greenwich. Some took luxury to the extreme, building homes that were replicas of European palaces like Marie Antoinette's Petit Trianon at Versailles or Warwick Castle in England. Private schools and country clubs began to appear in town, some of which continue to operate today.

In 1938 Connecticut historian Florence Crofut wrote that, "With its charming country and water views and proximity to New York, Greenwich has become a well-known residential section for antiquarians, authors, dramatists, educators, financiers, lawyers, and naturalists. Its spacious estates on a lovely waterfront have given it the name of 'America's finest residential town.'" More than seventy years later, it could be argued that Miss Crofut's assessment remains valid.

Greenwich was made even more convenient by the proliferation of automobiles and the construction of first the Merritt Parkway, then the Connecticut Turnpike, which served to carry an ever-increasing number of cars swiftly to and from metropolitan New York. The Turnpike, today Interstate 95, was the site of one of the grimmest tragedies in modern Greenwich history. In 1983 the bridge carrying I-95 over the Mianus River in Greenwich collapsed, killing three people.

Today, the number of internationally known writers, actors, singers, and celebrities from all walks of life who have a home in Greenwich runs into the dozens. In the latter decades of the twentieth century, Greenwich's nearness to New York reversed to a degree the relationship between the two. Many corporations have relocated their headquarters to Greenwich, and today thousands of employees commute there.

2.

STAMFORD

*I*rreconcilable differences motivated the first English settlers to migrate to Stamford from Wethersfield, Connecticut, in 1641. A disagreement over a religious issue, the specifics of which are lost to history, had so bitterly divided the Wethersfield Congregational church that at last a portion of the flock felt compelled to leave and strike out on their own.

Over the course of the next 150 years, Stamford developed into a community composed primarily of farmers. Any crops or livestock they raised beyond what they needed for their own use were shipped to New York City for sale.

In 1742, one of the first Church of England congregations in Connecticut, St. John's, was founded in Stamford. Doing so required courage and conviction. Connecticut's established, tax-supported religion was Congregationalism—the faith of the Puritans who had sought to "purify" that very same Church of England of what they considered corrupt, near-idolatrous rituals and symbols.

Hundreds of Stamford men fought in the war for American independence, including one of the first three recipients of the Purple Heart. Established by Gen. George Washington in 1782, the Purple Heart—literally a heart made out of purple cloth—was originally called the Badge of Military Merit. It was awarded not for wounds sustained in combat, but for "singularly meritorious action." Sgt. Daniel Brown of Stamford received the badge for his "great bravery, propriety, and deliberate firmness" in leading a potentially suicidal yet ultimately successful assault on a British defensive post at the Battle of Yorktown, Virginia.

The American Revolution was also a civil war, with many communities, neighbors, friends, and even families bitterly divided over whether to support independence or maintain allegiance to the British Crown. In Connecticut, most adherents to the king lived

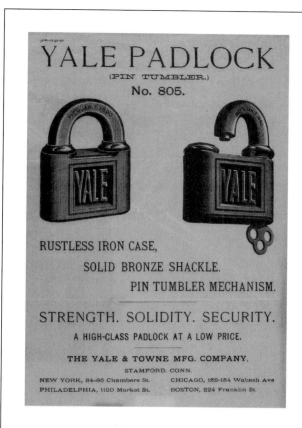

Yale padlock broadside, ca. 1890

Padlocks, like the one patented in 1890 featured in this advertisement, were among the many innovative security devices developed and manufactured by Yale & Towne during its ninety years in Stamford.

in the southwestern part of the state. The region had multiple ties to nearby New York, a stronghold of sentiment in favor of the Crown, and several congregations of the Church of England, which acknowledged the British monarch as its earthly head, were located there, including St. John's in Stamford.

Most Church of England members, including the pastor of St. John's, sided with the cause of independence. But dozens of Stamford Anglicans, as Church of England members were called, did choose to side with King George. Some of these Tories—or Loyalists, as they preferred to be known—left Stamford, and the Connecticut government confiscated their property. Stamford Loyalists often went to New York, which was controlled by the British from 1776 until 1783. Some went so far as to take up arms in support of the royal cause.

One example of how the war ruptured blood ties was the family of Samuel Jarvis. Jarvis was a well-regarded citizen of Stamford, having served as town clerk for many years. He was also an officer of St. John's Church. Upon the outbreak of hostilities between the

Southwest view of the borough of Stamford, ca. 1835

Stamford was a farming town of approximately 3,500 when this view of the borough portion, looking northeast across the Mill River in the foreground, was drawn around 1835. However, harbingers of its future as an industrial giant were already in evidence.

On the left is the smokestack of a "very extensive" iron foundry, possibly the Stamford Foundry Company, established in 1830 and in operation until 1954. To the right, between the two church spires, appears the mast of a vessel afloat on a just-completed canal running approximately half a mile from Stamford Harbor directly to Atlantic Square. At thirty feet wide and seven feet deep, the canal allowed schooners and sloops to sail right into the center of Stamford, where raw materials or finished products could be conveniently loaded or unloaded very close to a production facility.

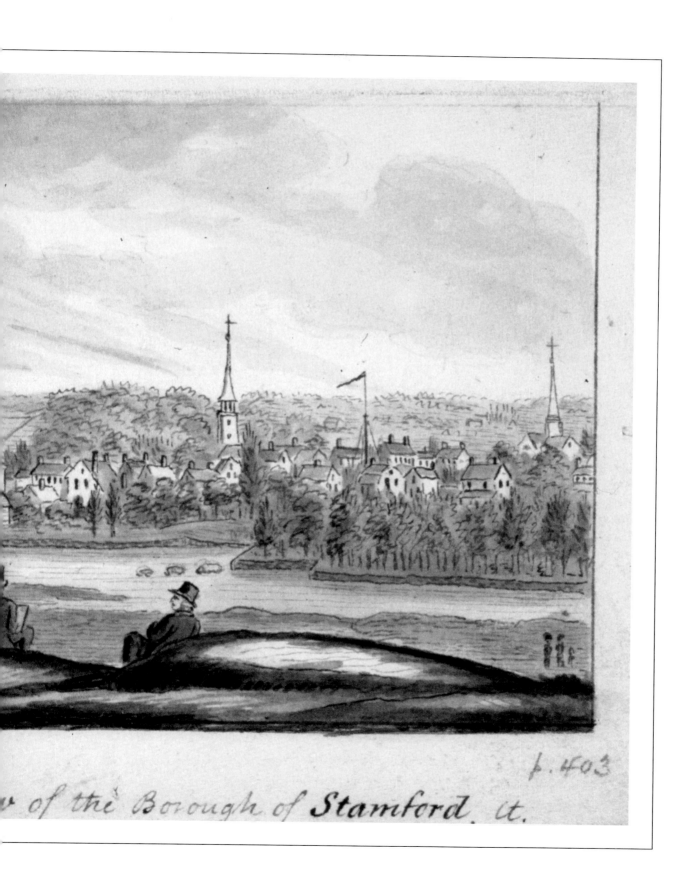

p. 403

...v of the Borough of Stamford. Ct.

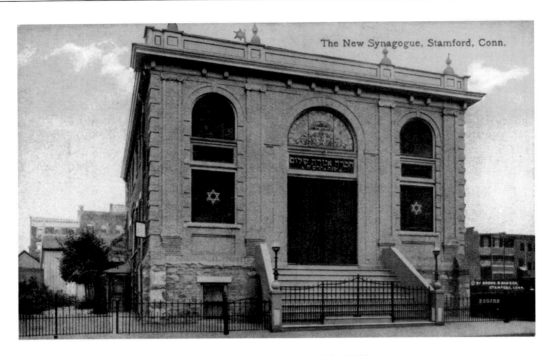

The New Synagogue, Stamford, Conn.

Congregation Agudath Sholom Synagogue, ca. 1904–1932

A small number of Jews had lived in Stamford since the early 1700s. But it was not until 1889 that the community had grown sufficiently big enough, due in large part to many recent immigrants from Russia, to establish the first organized institution, Congregation Agudath Sholom.

Stamford was home to close to two thousand Jews by the time Agudath Sholom built this synagogue on Greyrock Place in 1904. The building burned down in 1932 and was replaced by a synagogue on Grove Street.

British and colonists, local officials had Jarvis hauled before them as a suspected Loyalist. He eventually ended up in New York, where he died in 1780.

Of Jarvis's ten children, four sons sided with the Crown during the war, and two of his daughters also married Loyalists. When the defeated British evacuated New York in 1783, all six of the Loyalist Jarvis children migrated to Nova Scotia, where the Crown had granted land to colonists who had remained loyal.

In the decades following the Revolution, Stamford continued as primarily an agricultural town. It was drastically changed in one way during this period: It shrank geographically as the result of the northeastern portion being incorporated as the town of New Canaan in 1801, and the southeastern portion as the town of Darien in 1820.

But as the midpoint of the nineteenth century approached, Stamford, like much of Connecticut, began to experience new, exciting, sometimes unsettling developments that would make the agricultural village a nostalgic memory. A canal that provided an easy means of access from Stamford Harbor into the center of town was completed in 1833. The construction of a railroad line opened up a new avenue to the world beyond. Establishment of a regular train stop in Stamford in 1848 made it even easier to ship goods in and out, and for immigrants who arrived in the United States via New York City to make their way to Stamford.

A few industries developed in Stamford before the Civil War. Jobs in these factories were often filled by immigrants, primarily from Ireland. In 1840 there were few if any Irish in Stamford; by 1860 there were more than 1,200 natives of Ireland in a town of 7,200. The Civil War had just ended when Yale & Towne, the enterprise that would dominate the city's future for nearly a century, opened for business. The Yale of Yale & Towne was Linus Yale Jr., an ingenious locksmith. In 1868 he formed a partnership with Henry Towne to manufacture a lock patented by Yale with features that made it more secure and convenient than others on the market.

Neither Yale nor Towne hailed from Stamford, or even from Connecticut. They chose Stamford as the site for their new company because it offered several important advantages: the railroad, the canal, and hundreds of available employees, many of them immigrants or the children of immigrants.

Linus Yale died in 1868, but Henry Towne carried through with their plans. The plant opened in 1869 with thirty employees. It quickly became the city's biggest employer, with a workforce of 6,500 men and women by 1916. Stamford became known as the "Lock City," a nickname that today is commemorated on the town seal by two crossed Yale & Towne keys.

Yale & Towne was just one of the earliest chapters in the saga of Stamford's burgeoning into an industrial center. Both bicycles and automobiles were briefly made in Stamford. In the 1890s Stamford resident Charles Blickensderfer opened a factory to manufacture the typewriter he had patented. It would become the biggest producer of typewriters in the world. In 1919, Walter Bowes and Arthur Pitney, both of whom had been developing a postage meter, became partners. Their company, Pitney Bowes, became the world's biggest producer of postage meters.

Stamford, 1883

Stamford's development into a center of manufacturing was well under way by the time this bird's-eye view was published in 1883. The railroad had arrived, and Stamford had been made a regular stop in 1848. The width of the lower portion of the canal constructed in the early 1830s (seen at the center left) had been almost tripled, as well as deepened, to accommodate larger vessels and more of them.

Yale & Towne's lock factory, established a mere fourteen years earlier, had burgeoned into an extensive manufacturing complex. The variety of products turned out by Stamford factories at this point in time is reflected by other companies such as H. K. White's Straw Goods Manufactory, which turned out close to a million hats annually, and the Lincrusta-Walton Manufacturing Company, which produced a kind of "super" wallpaper, a thick covering that could be painted or stamped to look like wood or embossed leather. Other firms manufactured pumps, carriages, washing machines, and billiard tables.

Prosperous factory owners and managers built roomy, stylish homes on large, landscaped lots on the outskirts of the city, like those shown on Strawberry Hill Avenue in the right foreground. Located a short, convenient train ride from New York City, Stamford also became popular among wealthy Manhattanites as a site for summer estates.

Stamford, 1989

A photograph taken in 1989 from approximately the same vantage point of the artist who drew the ca. 1835 sketch demonstrates how completely Stamford had changed. The village of 1835, in which church steeples were the tallest structures, had vanished. The city of 1883 that had risen in its place, with its rapidly expanding factories, was gone as well. Stamford's skyline was now one of multilane highways and modern multistory office buildings. That trend has continued to the present, with construction of even larger headquarters facilities with price tags of hundreds of millions of dollars.

The Great Depression dealt a damaging, but by no means fatal, blow to Stamford's manufacturing. Although many companies that had been in business for decades closed their doors, new ones came in to replace them. In 1929 Jacob Schick opened a factory in Stamford to manufacture his newly patented electric razor. By 1940, the Schick Dry Shaver Company employed one thousand people.

Stamford's population grew in tandem with the proliferation of its industry, as immigrants arrived from an increasing array of countries, including Germany, Italy, and Russia, to fill the thousands of factory jobs. By 1910 a third of Stamford's residents had been born outside of the United States. Each decade saw breathtaking leaps in population. From 11,297 residents in 1880, Stamford's population increased nearly sevenfold, to 74,293 in 1950.

By the end of the Second World War, Stamford was still a city that made many things in large numbers for global markets. Manufacturing employed more Stamford workers than all other lines of work combined. But before another thirty years passed, the scenario would change drastically.

A slow exodus of manufacturers from Stamford began in the 1950s. Some firms shut down, while others left now-antiquated factories to relocate to areas where expenses were lower, regulations less strict, and labor unions less powerful. The Stamford Foundry Company closed in 1954 after 124 years in business. The Schick Dry Shaver Company left the following year. The Charles H. Phillips Company, which had been producing Milk of Magnesia in Stamford since the 1880s, closed its factory in 1976. But the most devastating loss by far was the shuttering in 1959 of the Yale & Towne factory. For the first time in more than a century, Stamford lost population, from 108,798 in 1970 to 102,453 in 1980.

Stamford was down but not out. It forged a new economic identity as home to the headquarters of dozens of global corporations. Major employers include General Electric Capital Corporation, Pitney Bowes, Xerox, and UBS Investment Bank. By 2005 manufacturing accounted for fewer than 10 percent of the jobs in the city. The population rebounded, increasing by more than 10 percent between 1980 and 2000. The "Lock City" had been transformed into "The City that Works."

3.

DARIEN

*D*arien, originally settled in the late 1600s as part of the town of Stamford, reportedly owes its existence as an independent town to the lethal cold of colonial winters. Connecticut law required all citizens to attend Sunday worship, which meant that every week Darien residents had to make the long trek on foot or horseback to the Congregational meetinghouse in Stamford.

In the 1730s, the deaths of several people attempting to get from Darien to Sabbath services prompted a movement for the establishment of a separate religious parish with its own meetinghouse. Middlesex Parish, which encompassed modern Darien, was created in 1737.

Frequently in Connecticut, establishment of a parish was the first step on the road to incorporation of a town. It was not until 1744, however, that a meetinghouse was finally constructed in Middlesex Parish. That year also saw the hiring of a Congregational minister, the Reverend Moses Mather. Southwestern Connecticut had more congregations of the Church of England than the rest of the colony. By the 1770s, Darien's population included an unusually high proportion of Anglicans, as Church of England members were called, estimated at more than 40 percent of families. That many Anglicans in a town in Congregational Connecticut spelled trouble when the American Revolution broke out, for the Church of England acknowledged the British monarch as its earthly leader, and the sympathies of many Anglicans tended to lie with the Crown.

Darien, on Long Island Sound and so close to British-controlled Long Island, endured repeated enemy raids during the Revolution. Often the raiders were former Darien residents, known as Loyalists, who had sided with the British in actual fighting of the war.

A prominent target of these raids was Rev. Mather, an outspoken advocate of American independence. On August 8, 1779, eight Loyalists, five of whom had previously

Fitch's Home, Noroton Heights, Conn.

Fitch's Home, Noroton Heights, ca. 1910

When the Civil War erupted in 1861, wealthy Darien merchant Benjamin Fitch was too old, at age sixty, to enlist in the ranks. He did the next best thing: He helped recruit Darien men for the Union Army with the promise that he would take care of their families.

Before the war was even over, Fitch had made good on his pledge. He donated five acres of land and $100,000—the equivalent of well over $1 million in 2007 dollars—for construction in Darien of "the first home for disabled war veterans and soldiers' orphans in the United States." The "Fitch Home" was dedicated on July 4, 1864.

Fitch bequeathed an additional $14,500 to the institution that bore his name upon his death in 1883. Five years later the State of Connecticut took over the home and operated it for the next half century. It was subsequently expanded to house a total of 750 veterans between the residence and hospital.

In 1930 the Fitch Home had more than three hundred residents. Just two years later the economic hardship of the Great Depression had caused that number to more than triple to one thousand. Fitch Home residents made up approximately 8 percent of Darien's entire population.

The Fitch Home closed in 1940, when its residents moved to the brand-new veterans' home built by the state in Rocky Hill. In the 1950s the Darien complex was renovated to serve as apartments.

Southwestern view of the Congregational Church, Darien, ca. 1835

No place in Darien was safe during the civil war that was the American Revolution—not even a church pew or pulpit on the Sabbath. Rev. Moses Mather was conducting services in the Darien Congregational meetinghouse on the afternoon of Sunday, July 22, 1781, when a band of about forty Loyalists, led by a former Darien resident, surrounded the building. A few worshipers managed to escape through the windows, but the remaining male members of the congregation, more than three dozen, along with Rev. Mather, sixty-two, were rounded up, tied together, and hustled off to the shore, where they were put on board boats and taken across the Sound to Long Island.

Some of the captives were released not long after, but twenty-seven, including Rev. Mather, were held prisoner by the British for five months. They were incarcerated on the notorious prison ships and in the Provost Prison—infamous as hellholes rife with filth, disease, and vermin, where men suffered from insufficient food, heat, medical care, and sanitary facilities.

Nineteen of the Darien captives lived to finally be released on December 17, 1781, in a prisoner exchange. The survivors had to walk home to Darien from New York in the winter. One young man, James Bell, died along the way.

lived in Darien, invaded Rev. Mather's home and took the minister and three of his sons captive.

The four were imprisoned in New York, where Moses Mather Jr., nineteen, died on September 22. His father and two brothers were exchanged not long afterward. However, Rev. Mather would find himself a British prisoner a second time before the end of the Revolution in 1783. Despite his ordeals, Rev. Mather continued as minister of the Darien Congregational Church until his death in 1806 at the age of eighty-seven. He had been pastor for sixty-two years.

In 1820, after several years of determined agitation, Middlesex Parish was at last incorporated as a separate town from Stamford. Residents now confronted a fresh decision: what to name their new town.

1272   Congregational Church, Darien, Conn.

Congregational church, ca. 1920-1930

Darien's original Congregational meetinghouse, built in 1744, was replaced after more than ninety years of service. It was razed, and in 1836 the current brick meetinghouse was erected on a site next to the original one.

Middlesex seems not to have been considered as a possible option. Some residents wanted to call it Belltown or Bellville, after Thaddeus Bell, the state representative who had determinedly pressed the issue of incorporation to its successful conclusion. When Bell turned down the honor, he was asked to make his own suggestion. Tradition says the name for the new town was provided by a sailor of Bell's acquaintance, recently returned from a voyage to the Isthmus of Panama, then known as the Isthmus of Darien. The friend purportedly saw similarities between the new town's location between the bigger communities of Norwalk and Stamford, and that of the Isthmus of Darien between the Atlantic and Pacific oceans. Darien it was.

The railroad arrived in Darien in 1848. Two years later the town's population of 1,454 included nearly one hundred Irish immigrants, most of whom had probably come to work on building the railroad.

Harvesting of oysters, clams, and lobsters was a thriving business in Darien during the nineteenth century. But little in the way of manufacturing was ever established, a pattern that persisted in the wake of the Civil War. Instead, wealthy residents began building large homes, and New Yorkers erected summer houses at spots along the shore. As the development of large-scale industry turned neighboring Stamford into a densely populated city, Darien evolved into a bedroom community for families whose breadwinners commuted via train to white-collar jobs elsewhere, primarily in Manhattan.

More than half a dozen residential developments transformed Darien farmland into upscale homes prior to World War II. Clubs were established to cater to the hunters, golfers, and yachtsmen among the new residents. The Wee Burn Country Club, in existence since 1895, was the first golf club in Connecticut and one of the earliest to be established in the United States.

A 1935 historical publication declared proudly that "Darien has become noted for the number of its clubs of various kinds, which have drawn many persons to it, and for the excellence of its school system . . . [and] its splendid trees and charm of landscape. As a result persons of wealth and culture have been drawn to it in large numbers, have purchased land and erected homes, and have become a part of its fine community life." That appeal had resulted in a doubling of Darien's population between 1920 and 1940, from 4,184 to 9,222. A number of households had live-in servants, many of them immigrants from more than a dozen countries, from Finland to Japan to the West Indies.

The Club House at Tokeneke Beach, ca. 1907–1909

The Tokeneke Beach Club, founded in 1907, was one of several private recreational establishments started in Darien during the first decades of the twentieth century. The clubhouse and pier on which people of all ages lounge, in this postcard view that dates from early in the club's history, burned down in 1932.

Still to come was the advent of the automobile, which freed commuters from the tyranny of train timetables. Completion of the Merritt Parkway in 1940 and of the Connecticut Turnpike in the 1950s made travel between Darien and Manhattan even more convenient. Again, population doubled between 1940 and 1960, when it reached 18,437. It has increased very slowly since, now exceeding twenty thousand.

Darien today is one of the wealthiest communities in America—and one of the most expensive places to live. The town's grand list is topped by two country clubs. The median household income in 2007 was $181,821—more than twice that of Fairfield County, and nearly three times that of the state as a whole.

4.

NORWALK

*O*n the evening of Sunday, July 11, 1779, Norwalk was a blackened, smoldering ruin. The fires that had devastated the town had been started not by lightning or human carelessness; they had been deliberately set by enemy British raiders to destroy food and war materiel stockpiled at Norwalk for the soldiers fighting for American independence—and to teach residents an unforgettable lesson about the penalty for rebelling against the British Crown.

It was a low point—perhaps the lowest—in Norwalk's more than 350 years of history. Some residents would leave to start fresh on western frontier lands offered as compensation for their losses, but many more remained and resolutely set about rebuilding their homes, shops, and churches, establishing the foundation for modern Norwalk, a city of eighty-five thousand that is home to the headquarters of more than a dozen national and international firms.

Norwalk was settled around 1649 and incorporated as a town in 1651. A Congregational church was established the following year, and in 1737 St. Paul's, a parish of the Church of England, was founded.

In 1754 Norwalk native Thomas Fitch was elected governor of the Colony of Connecticut. He was still in office eleven years later, in 1765, when the first in the series of major political controversies that would culminate in the American Revolution occurred: the Stamp Act. The British Parliament passed the Stamp Act in order to levy taxes on paper used in the colonies. Payment of the tax was demonstrated by a stamp attached to the paper. News of this new tax, imposed without their consent, infuriated colonists up and down the Atlantic coast.

Although Governor Fitch personally opposed the legislation, he felt duty bound to support it—for which he was burned in effigy in Hartford. Worse was in store for Fitch. In

Loyalist officer's uniform coat, ca. 1776–1779

Norwalk had more Loyalists than almost any Connecticut town; estimates put the number at one out of every four residents. Documentation exists to prove that more than one hundred residents were prosecuted or lost property for having remained faithful to King George III.

Loyalists who took up arms on behalf of the Crown included Monson Hoyt of Norwalk, who enlisted as a lieutenant in a Loyalist unit, the Prince of Wales American Regiment, on April 6, 1777. This red wool coat was part of Hoyt's officer's uniform in the Prince of Wales Regiment.

Hoyt served in the king's forces until the end of the Revolution in 1783. He was among the thousands of Loyalists who sailed from New York to Nova Scotia, where they could take up grants of land awarded by the British government as reward for their fidelity and in partial compensation for property lost as a result.

Unlike most Loyalists who removed to Canada, Monson Hoyt didn't remain there. He returned to the United States—not to his native Connecticut, but to nearby New York. In 1792 he married Lucretia Hammond of Long Island, and in 1800 he was living in New York City. He died in 1805.

Clam Potpie redware plate, ca. 1830–1850

The Smith Pottery was one of Norwalk's most successful potteries for more than half a century. The firm had its origins in the pottery started by Asa Smith Sr. in 1825. Three of Smith's sons eventually joined the company, which at its peak had as many as fifty workers turning out several types of pottery that were marketed throughout much of the United States.

The Smith pottery made large quantities of redware, so called because during firing the clay turned a dark brownish red, a color that deepened over time. A distinctive feature of Smith redware is simple decoration or words in a flowing cursive that personalize the piece with a name, or sometimes, as in the case of this plate made between 1830 and 1850, the use for which the piece was intended. The words were created by dribbling diluted clay—called "slip," hence the term "slipware"—on the surface of a piece of pottery before it was fired or glazed—much like writing on a cake with a tube of frosting.

Glass and metal replaced pottery as the preferred material for containers and cookware in the later 1800s. Asa Smith Jr. sold his family's pottery in 1888 but continued to manage it for a number of years.

Eastern view of the village of Old Well, Norwalk, South Norwalk, ca. 1835

Smoke billowing into the sky signaled the significant economic progress South Norwalk had made by the 1830s. The plume to the left emanates from a steamboat, a form of transportation barely twenty years old, which made a regular run several times a week between Norwalk and New York City. The others rise from several of the town's flourishing potteries and hat factories. This view, from a spot on the east bank of the Norwalk River near Washington Street, looks west toward where the Norwalk Maritime Center stands today.

...lage of **Old Well**, *Norwalk Con.*

South view of Norwa

South view of Norwalk, ca. 1835

The site where the Norwalk River narrows and Wall Street crosses it on a bridge looked like this in early 1835. The rise at the extreme right topped by trees is Grumman's Hill. General Tryon, commander of the British attack on Norwalk in 1779, set up his field headquarters on this eminence and issued orders for torching the village down below. Grumman's Hill has long since been leveled.

The extent to which Norwalk had rebuilt itself half a century after the devastation is evident in the structures visible. In addition to St. Peter's Episcopal Church next to Grumman's Hill, and the First Congregational Church next to it, the Town House, used for official town business, had been built in 1794.

By 1835, however, the Town House shown here "had long been in a ruinous state, and much disfigured the appearance of the place," according to historian John Warner Barber. A group of local residents who got tired of waiting for officials to replace the eyesore tore it down on a night in July of 1835 and placed the ruins at the side of the road. A new brick town house, built the next year, still stands today as part of the Mill Hill Historic Park maintained by the Norwalk Historical Society.

1766 he was defeated for reelection, an almost unheard-of occurrence in Connecticut, the "Land of Steady Habits," where the governor, once in office, was typically reelected until he died or decided not to run again.

When actual war between Great Britain and its colonies broke out in 1775, it was not long before Norwalk felt the effects. The main theater of war shifted from Boston to Manhattan in the spring of 1776, after which the British inflicted a series of crushing defeats on the Continental Army. Following one of these losses, the Battle of White Plains, New York, on October 28, 1776, several hundred wounded soldiers arrived in Norwalk in need of medical care.

At the same time, hundreds of Norwalk residents who sympathized with the king in the Revolution were fleeing town, many taking refuge on British-controlled Manhattan or Long Island. Stephen Hoyt, a Norwalk Tory—or Loyalist, as those who remained faithful to the Crown preferred to be called—recruited a full company of men willing to take up arms for the king in the Prince of Wales American Regiment of Loyalists.

Norwalk also suffered periodic raids by British and Loyalists from bases on Long Island, just a few short miles across the Sound. Then the unthinkable occurred.

British General William Tryon, who despised Connecticut patriots for what he called their "ingenious and wanton insurrection," had spent a week in early July of 1779 mounting amphibious assaults on several towns along the Connecticut coast, destroying supplies intended for the Continental Army and fulfilling his orders to inflict "all injury consistent with humanity." Norwalk was the last target in this spree of deadly devastation.

By the time Tryon's fleet, carrying 2,600 British, Hessian, and Loyalist troops, appeared off the coast of Norwalk on July 10, residents knew that Fairfield had been put to the torch by the enemy the previous day. Townspeople hid their valuables and fled farther inland to what they hoped would be safety.

The first wave of enemy invaders began marching up the eastern bank of the Norwalk River before dawn. They soon seized control of the village center area, site of the town house and the First Congregational and St. Paul's Anglican churches. A second wave headed up the western bank a few hours later, setting fire to houses, barns, and stores along the way, including in the village of South Norwalk.

A hastily assembled force of approximately nine hundred American soldiers attempted to repel the invaders but ultimately had to retreat. The British torched the village center, destroying dozens of buildings and both churches. They at last retreated back down the eastern bank, setting fire to more buildings as they passed. Several Loyalists took the opportunity to leave with the retreating raiders.

The destruction inflicted by the British raid was staggering: Eighty homes, eighty-seven barns, two houses of worship, seventeen shops, four mills, and five ships had gone up in flames. Only six houses were left standing—purportedly because they belonged to Loyalists.

Norwalk recovered slowly. A decade after the attack the chimneys of houses burned in the raid stood like scabs on still unhealed wounds. St. Paul's rebuilt its church by 1785, but a new Congregational meetinghouse wasn't completed until 1794. Eventually the State of Connecticut compensated more than three hundred residents for their losses. In 1792 the state also designated half a million acres to which it held title in northeastern Ohio for land grants to victims of the British coastal attacks. The area was called the Firelands, for the flames that had devastated so many lives in Connecticut.

Following the war's end in 1783, thousands of Loyalists sailed from New York to Nova Scotia, where the British Crown offered them grants of land in thanks for their loyalty. However, some Norwalk Loyalists wanted to come back to the town they had once called home. Initially residents weren't in a forgiving mood, but resentment softened with the passage of time, and some Norwalk Loyalists were able to return.

Beginning in 1790, Norwalk became a center of maritime trade with ports along the Atlantic coast and in the West Indies. Shipyards sprang up, as did shops to turn out all the supplies needed for building and sailing vessels.

Norwalk shrank geographically in the early 1800s. A portion became part of the new town of New Canaan in 1801. The next year most of the new town of Wilton was taken from Norwalk. Finally, in 1835, part of Norwalk was included in the newly incorporated town of Westport.

By the 1830s, Norwalk was at last well on the way to recovery. Beyond the flourishing maritime trade, the manufacture of pottery and especially hats played a major role in the town's economic rebound.

At least half a dozen hat factories operated in South Norwalk in 1836. By 1885 there were a dozen, with more than two thousand workers, making hatting Norwalk's most important industry, and one that would endure well into the twentieth century.

Bell Island 1884

Potters had begun working in Norwalk before 1800. They produced several different varieties of pottery primarily for practical purposes, including water coolers that were exported to the West Indies, oyster jars to hold the catch of local oystermen, and plates that were sold through much of the eastern United States. By 1835 there were at least half a dozen operating, most in Old Well, today's South Norwalk. The most successful

East Beach, Bell Island, Norwalk, 1884

Sightseeing, rather than swimming, seems to be the goal of this group at East Beach at Bell Island in 1884, judging from the binoculars one man is using. Bell Island, in the Rowayton section of Norwalk, was developed by New Yorkers and well-to-do residents of Danbury into a summer resort with cottages like those in the background, boating, and a beach.

of Norwalk potteries, however, that run by Asa Smith and later his sons, was located at the foot of Mill Hill.

One of the nation's most important oyster industries developed in Norwalk during the late 1800s and continued into the early twentieth century. Oysters were shipped to markets in New York, on the West Coast, and to Europe.

Spectators on bicycle racecourse, East Norwalk, ca. 1898

Spectators wait along the course of what seems like Victorian Norwalk's mini version of the Tour de France, a bicycle race from the lower end of the town green to Gregory's Point. The distance between the two sites is approximately three miles as the crow flies, but the route the cyclists had to follow along the streets was undoubtedly considerably longer.

Construction of a rail line through Norwalk in 1848 opened up the town to immigration, and by 1870 there were more than 1,400 Irish-born residents in Norwalk. Companies making everything from cigars to corsets to shirts joined the hatters, potters, and oystermen of Norwalk in the late 1800s. Following the turn of the twentieth century, immigrants came by the hundreds from many other countries, including Hungary, Germany, Italy, and Poland.

Pottery declined as an important industry in the late 1800s, with the advent of glass and steel used for containers. Several of the major Norwalk hat firms were purchased in the 1930s by the Hat Company of America, which continued to operate its enterprise in Norwalk. However, hats were slowly declining in popularity, and by the 1960s they were no longer an essential or even a common part of the average American's wardrobe. The Hat Company of America moved its manufacturing to Tennessee.

Norwalk's greatest leap in population occurred between 1940, when the population was approximately forty thousand, and 1970, when it was seventy-nine thousand. The baby boom and suburbanization had caused the number of residents to nearly double in thirty years.

The 1970s saw the inauguration of the South Norwalk Revitalization Project. The keystone was the Maritime Aquarium at Norwalk, which opened in 1988 and today attracts more than half a million visitors a year. Also drawing on Norwalk's connection to the sea, the Norwalk Seaport Association has held an annual Oyster Festival since 1978, with an average annual attendance of approximately one hundred thousand. Today Tallmadge Brothers of South Norwalk is the country's biggest commercial oystering outfit.

Modern Norwalk is a city of approximately eighty-five thousand. Most of the industries that once dominated the economy are gone, but today Norwalk is home to corporate headquarters of more than a dozen national or international companies.

5.

WESTPORT

*T*ake a slice of Fairfield, Norwalk, and Weston. Combine. The result in 1835 was the brand-new town of Westport.

People had been living in what today makes up Westport for nearly two centuries. English settlement began in the late 1640s at the Green's Farms area near Long Island Sound. A Congregational meetinghouse was built in 1711 at Green's Farms, which for more than a century was the center of community life.

The American Revolution delivered death and destruction directly to Westport's door on two occasions. The first occurred in the spring of 1777. Late in the day on April 25, approximately 1,800 British troops disembarked from two dozen vessels at Compo Beach. With midnight approaching, they set out on their mission: destruction of a large store of patriot supplies at Danbury, twenty-two miles away. As the enemy soldiers marched along Compo Road, they set fire to houses and barns.

Two days later, returning from their mission—which they had accomplished despite encountering significant resistance from patriot defenders—the British approached Compo Beach, with patriot forces in hot pursuit. The local militia were waiting for them.

The British retreat brought them to the summit of Compo Hill. The Americans confronted and pushed back the British, who by now were almost out of ammunition. The redcoats mounted a last, desperate bayonet charge against the patriots, forcing them to retreat and buying enough time for the British to get back onto their transport ships.

Two years later, the British returned to Westport on another mission of destruction. In the early days of July of 1779 enemy troops had disembarked from British vessels to burn and plunder coastal towns, including Norwalk and Fairfield. On July 8 the redcoats torched the Congregational meetinghouse at Green's Farms, but they failed to make off with the communion silver thanks to the quick thinking of Deacon Ebenezer Jesup, who concealed it in his well.

"Minute Man," Westport, Conn.

406422

Minute Man, ca. 1910

Dedicated in 1910, the Minute Man statue honors the dozens of patriots who fell resisting the British invasion and attack on Danbury in April of 1777 that both began and ended at Compo Beach, where the monument stands. The statue is by American sculptor H. Daniel Webster, whose work also can be found in the National Statuary Hall Collection in the U.S. Capitol building. Webster used several men descended from local families as models for the statue.

Following the American Revolution, Westport developed a brisk trade with the West Indies and with ports along the Atlantic coast. A bridge was built across the Saugatuck River, then the boundary of Norwalk and Fairfield. Wharves, warehouses, and stores to accommodate the shipping activity sprang up on both banks of the river at this point, resulting in the development of the village of Saugatuck. By the 1830s, Saugatuck had become the center of community life in Westport, boasting both a new Congregational meetinghouse and an Episcopal church.

In 1835 the new town of Westport was incorporated. Approximately 800 people lived in the part of Fairfield that merged into Westport, 725 in the part of Norwalk, and 170 in that of Weston, for a total population of about 1,700.

Exhibition of fireworks! On the evening of the Fourth of July, 1860

The extravaganza of Independence Day fireworks advertised in this broadside was sponsored by Richard Henry Winslow at the grand home he called Compo House, which stood at the corner of Post Road East and Compo Road North. Richard Winslow was a founder of the banking firm Winslow, Lanier & Company in New York City, who moved to Westport sometime in the 1850s.

Health problems had caused Winslow to step down from his financial business sometime around 1859, when he was barely past fifty years old. In 1860, the year he presented this Fourth of July light show, he was listed in the census as a "farmer," owning real estate and personal property valued at a total of $200,000—more than $4 million in modern dollars.

Winslow did not have the opportunity to enjoy Compo House for long. He died in February of 1861.

In the ensuing decades, onions became a staple of Westport's economy. The town actually became the nation's leading grower of the vegetable. With the outbreak of the Civil War, onion cultivation became an even more lucrative line of work. Westport became the

84.

view in the central part of W.

tport, Con.   p. 4

View in the central part of Westport, ca. 1835

The center of Westport as it looked around 1835, the year of its birth as an independent town, is seen from the eastern bank of the Saugatuck River. The bridge over the Saugatuck linked the two halves of what was then called Saugatuck Village.

The view was up-to-date. The large building with the square tower seen in the left background is the newly constructed Christ Church, which had been consecrated on November 2, 1835. Today this image graces the town seal of Westport.

South view of Saugatuck Bridge and village between Fairfield and Norwalk, ca. 1835

The bridge that since the early 1800s had served as the connection between the parts of Norwalk and Fairfield that would be included in the new town of Westport is seen in this view, looking north along the Saugatuck River. Saugatuck Village, as the spot where the bridge crossed was known, had developed into a bustling community during the decades following the American Revolution, largely as the result of trade conducted by vessels like those depicted on the river.

The steeple to the far right belongs to the Saugatuck Congregational Church, established in 1832. That meetinghouse still stands, a few hundred yards to the east of its original location, at 275 Post Road East, to which site it was moved in 1950.

South view of Sau
Fair

atuc Bridge and village between ...eld and Norwalk.

Ethel Smith Atwell and Cyril William Tolley, Westport, 1936

Celebrity sightings are nothing new in Westport. In 1936 Cyril William Tolley, two-time winner of the British Amateur Golfing Championship, and Ethel Smith Atwell, recently divorced from well-known actor and comedian Roy Atwell, came to Westport to be married. When they discovered that Connecticut had a five-day waiting period before a wedding could be conducted, they spent the time in lighthearted frolicking, including posing in the window of a local tavern.

biggest source of onions for the Union Army, which included them pickled in the troop's rations to help prevent scurvy. But before the end of the nineteenth century, Westport's onion bonanza fell victim to cutworms.

By the middle of the nineteenth century Westport had begun to attract summer visitors. The first were former residents who had moved to New York City or migrated to western frontiers, and were seeking a place to stay when they returned for a visit to the old hometown. Boardinghouses were soon joined by establishments such as the Phipps Hotel, built in 1864. Later known as the Beachside Inn, it operated into the twentieth century.

The early 1900s saw an influx of summer visitors to Westport. Cottages began to proliferate on Compo Beach in the 1920s. Among the vacationers and new residents were artists and writers who arrived in increasing numbers as the decades passed. The opening of the Westport Country Playhouse in 1931 in a century-old converted barn began attracting the famous and soon-to-be famous of stage and screen to town, from Paul Robeson to Henry Fonda, from Ethel Barrymore to Liza Minnelli. Many productions staged in Westport went on to Broadway, including two classics that had their world premieres at the playhouse: *Come Back, Little Sheba* and *The Trip to Bountiful*. Today the playhouse is one of America's finest regional theatres.

Long before Ronald Reagan and Arnold Schwarzenegger moved from the soundstage to the political arena, a Westport resident made the transition from Hollywood actor to governor. John Lodge made twenty-one movies in Hollywood, including *Little Women* with Katharine Hepburn in 1933 and *The Little Colonel* with Shirley Temple in 1935. Lodge chose Westport as his home when he left show business. In 1950 he was elected governor of Connecticut and was reelected to a second term in 1952.

Westport experienced the powerful impact of the post–World War II baby boom and suburbanization. The town's population grew from 11,667 in 1950 to 20,955 in 1960 and to 27,318 in 1970. So intense was the resulting demand for housing that many summer cottages were upgraded and converted into year-round residences.

Those new residents have included a host of wealthy and talented individuals attracted by Westport's easy access to New York and its quality of life. Westporters have included everyone from science fiction author Rod Serling to domestic doyenne Martha Stewart, from Bette Davis to Paul Newman, from Neil Sedaka to Michael Bolton.

TRAVELING UP AND DOWN THE COAST

Rivers and Long Island Sound were the primary highways for the first two centuries after English settlement of the coast. Traveling via boat was far easier than trying to traverse the crude ruts that passed for roads until the mid-1800s. Vessels of many different sizes and designs could rely on the current or the wind for power, or, failing those, men pulling on oars.

Steamer City of Hartford

"Steamer City of Hartford," 1867. By the latter half of the nineteenth century, steamboats that would have done the Mississippi River proud, like the *City of Hartford,* shown in 1867, were a key component of transportation along the Connecticut coast. Steamboats, like railroads, would ultimately fall victim to the automobile.

New Haven and Northampton daily canal boat: freight tariff, 1844. The idea of creating water routes that would run where man wanted them to go, rather than where nature had arbitrarily placed them, generated great interest in the early 1800s. The phenomenal success of the man-made Erie Canal, opened in 1825 to transport people and products between Albany and Buffalo, New York, heightened enthusiasm for similar projects to a near frenzy in many states, including Connecticut.

New Haven business leaders developed a project to construct a canal from their city north to Northampton, Massachusetts, on the Connecticut River. Such a waterway would, they hoped, give New Haven a competitive edge over towns along the Connecticut River, by providing a direct access route down which the bounty of the farms and workshops of interior Connecticut, of Massachusetts, and of regions farther north could flow into the port city of New Haven.

Called the Farmington Canal because it would run through the town of Farmington, the project was organized in 1822, and construction began in 1825. Laborers dug the canal with shovels, and progress was slow but steady. The entire canal between New Haven and Northampton was finally completed in 1835.

The illustration on this announcement of freight charge shows how the canals served as a means of transportation. Canal boats were hitched to teams of horses that walked on paths on the edge of the canal, pulling the boats along.

As the broadside also shows, the cost of shipping goods via canal was not cheap, with fees in the neighborhood of $3—the equivalent of $80 or more in modern money—to ship a thousand brooms or a ton of dried fish. Thirteen years later the Farmington Canal was bankrupt and out of business. The cost of operating and maintaining the waterway continually exceeded income; ultimately more than $2 million was poured into the canal project—the rough equivalent of $54 million today. The Farmington Canal had been not just the proverbial dollar short, but a day late: Barely had it opened when the first railroad line in Connecticut was laid down in 1837. Rails were superior in almost every way to canals; they cost less to build and maintain, could go almost anywhere, and could move goods faster and less expensively.

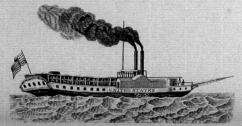

New-York and New-Haven.

STEAM-BOAT DAILY LINE.

THE STEAM-BOATS

United States, *Capt. Beecher,*

AND

Providence, *Capt. Sanford,*

HAVE commenced their regular trips, and will continue to run through the season, between *New-Haven* and *New-York*, in the following order, viz.

One of said Boats will be dispatched from *New-Haven* every evening at 7 o'clock, and one from *New-York*, (foot of Maiden-lane,) every morning, at the same hour, Sundays excepted. Two extra trips in each week will also be performed, a Boat leaving *New-York* on Saturdays, at 4 o'clock, P. M. and *New-Haven* on Mondays, at 9 o'clock, A. M.

POST COACHES

Will always be in readiness, on the arrival of the Boats at New-Haven, to convey passengers immediately on to Hartford, Boston and Providence---on Mondays, Wednesdays and Fridays, by the way of Middletown, and on Tuesdays, Thursdays and Saturdays, by Meriden and Berlin.

The MAIL STAGE for *Hartford*, by *Middletown*, also leaves New-Haven every evening at 10 o'clock, and an **ACCOMMODATION STAGE** for Hartford will also leave New-Haven every morning, Sundays excepted. By this route the passage from New-York to Hartford is usually performed five to six hours sooner than by any other route.

   ☞ Passengers travelling eastward, will breakfast and dine on board the Boats, and, if they choose, sup at Hartford, where they will arrive within fifteen hours from the time of departure from New-York, in season for a comfortable night's rest, and to take the early Stages from Hartford.
   Freight received on board at moderate prices. For information relative to freight or passage, apply to the Captains on board, or, at the Steam-Boat Office, head of Long-Wharf, New-Haven, to

JOEL ROOT, *Agent.*

   N. B. *All Goods, Baggage and Specie, at the risk of the owners thereof.*

New-Haven, April 6, 1826.

New York and New Haven steamboat daily line, 1826. Steam-powered boats began operating on Long Island Sound during the second decade of the nineteenth century. By 1826 steamboats were making regularly scheduled runs between New Haven and New York.

Carriage, ca. 1800, DETAIL. Human and horsepower were the only options for overland travel along the coast for the first two centuries after English settlement. The carriage depicted in this list of fees for passage on the Hartford and New Haven Turnpike around 1800 would have been one of the more luxurious vehicles of its time.

Pequot Wheel Club, New London, ca. 1900. The first bicycles manufactured in the United States came out of a factory in Hartford in 1878. The foot-powered vehicles were extremely popular and spawned a number of cycling groups, like New London's Pequot Wheel Club, shown around 1900.

Horse-drawn omnibus, Stamford, 1894. Trolleys, or streetcars, that ran on tracks laid down the middle of roads began to appear along the shoreline in the mid-1800s, and they would remain a key component of local transportation well into the twentieth century. First pulled by horses, like this one-car "omnibus" in Stamford in 1894, they were later electrified.

Streetcars made it possible for people to live farther than walking distance from their place of work, contributing to the development of residential neighborhoods on the outskirts of cities. They made day trips into city centers for shopping or entertainment convenient. And streetcars were an important element in the development of the shoreline's recreation industry, for they made it possible for individuals of even modest means to get away to spend a day at beaches, picnic grounds, and especially amusement parks.

HARTFORD

AND

NEW-HAVEN

RAIL-ROAD.

On the 4th of July, the Cars

Will leave Hartford for New Haven, at 8 o'clock, A. M.
"   "   "   10 3-4   "
"   "   "   6   P. M.

Will leave New-Haven for Hartford, at 8 o'clock, A. M.
"   "   "   11 1-2   "
"   "   "   6   P. M.

HARTFORD, July 1st, 1842.

Hartford and New Haven Railroad broadside, July 4, 1842. The first steam-powered train operated in Connecticut in 1837 in Stonington, and a mere five years later a rail line connected Hartford and New Haven. Railroad tracks would expand throughout Connecticut, the shoreline included, with amazing speed, making overland transportation faster, more convenient, and more affordable than what could have been imagined even as late as the 1820s.

Train travel connected communities along the coast to each other, to the rest of the state, then to the region, and ultimately the nation. It opened up an entire world for shoreline residents and had an impact on nearly every facet of daily existence, including commerce, culture, recreation, and education. It also greatly altered the quality and pace of life. The railroad would dominate surface transportation in Connecticut for nearly a century. It remains more important along the coast than in other parts of the state due to commuter trains and Amtrak.

Pope Company outing, Savin Rock excursion, West Haven, 1905. Automobiles began appearing on Connecticut roads at the dawn of the twentieth century, and nothing along the coast would ever be the same. This collection of cars, produced by the Pope Manufacturing Company of Hartford and assembled for a company outing at West Haven's Savin Rock in 1905, was among the first of a wave of automobiles that would proliferate, changing everything even more profoundly than trains had in the decades preceding the Civil War.

Cars provided a degree of personal freedom unparalleled in human history. Whether heading just a few blocks away or setting out on a long trip, people were no longer constrained by the time-tables, schedules, or limited routes of trains or trolleys. They could come and go as they pleased, with a speed and convenience that no other form of land transportation could match. Individuals could live farther than ever before from their workplace and could act on the impulse to go to the beach or the amusement park. Improvements in local roads, and ultimately the construction first of the Merritt Parkway, then the Connecticut Turnpike, made travel by car faster and easier than ever.

Automobiles had largely surpassed trains and trolleys for transporting passengers by the middle of the twentieth century. Not long afterward, trucks supplanted railroad boxcars for shipping all manner of goods.

However, automobiles were definitely a mixed blessing for towns along the Connecticut coast. Small communities that had not changed significantly for generations suddenly had paved roads down which buzzed noisy, exhaust-spewing vehicles at all hours of the day and night. The tempo of life accelerated, and some of the charm rubbed off communities that had looked and functioned the same for decades, if not centuries. More and more not-so-desirable changes were made to accommodate the growing numbers of cars: parking lots, traffic signals, gas stations. Thousands of people all trying to travel to a beach or an amusement park by car created traffic jams and parking nightmares. Cities lost population as people moved to suburbs that had become feasible places to reside thanks to the quick, convenient commute made possible by the automobile.

Construction of limited-access highways like the Merritt Parkway and particularly the Connecticut Turnpike relieved some of the stress on overburdened roads that had originally been laid out for horses. But many small towns lost the commuter traffic that had been an important part of their retail business base, forcing some into economic stagnation.

Bridge on the Merritt Parkway, 1930s. Completed in 1940, the Merritt Parkway, stretching from the New York border in Greenwich to the Housatonic River in Stratford, was a transportation improvement, an aesthetic accomplishment, and a work of art. Primarily intended to help relieve automobile congestion on Fairfield County roads, it was also developed with the goal of creating something attractive. The parkway's thirty-seven miles were laid out so as to create a relatively undeveloped, unspoiled driving experience. Each of the sixty-nine bridges built to carry a road over the parkway was designed as a unique creation by architect George Dunkelberger, who used a variety of styles popular during the 1930s, including Art Deco.

6.

FAIRFIELD

Fairfield founding father Roger Ludlow was on a mission of war when he first saw the pleasant land to which he would guide English settlers. It was the summer of 1637, and Ludlow was one of the leaders of a force of three hundred English soldiers who, along with a number of Mohegan Indians, were pursuing fleeing Pequot Indians who had managed to avoid being slaughtered in a surprise attack by English forces on their village at Groton in eastern Connecticut in May. The English and Mohegans caught up with the Pequots on July 13, 1637, in the Great Swamp in the Southport section of Fairfield. Only about one hundred of the Native Americans survived the ensuing battle, which all but destroyed the Pequot people.

Ludlow was back two years later with a band of men who established the community they called Fairfield, for its extensive salt marshes and open fields—cleared by local Native Americans who had recently succumbed to disease. The land lived up to its name over the course of the next century and more. Local farms produced fine crops that included wheat and flax, which, along with livestock and lumber, were often shipped from Black Rock Harbor, then part of Fairfield, to towns on the Atlantic coast, the West Indies, and even Europe. Shipbuilding became an important part of the economy as well.

But amid the prosperity, Fairfield had dark moments during its first 150 years. In 1651 a local woman, Goody Bassett, was hanged after being convicted of witchcraft charges. Three years later another woman, Goody Knapp, followed her to the gallows on the same charge. And during the American Revolution, in one twenty-four-hour period, a brutal enemy wrought death and destruction upon Fairfield on a massive scale, reducing much of the town to ashes and rubble.

On July 7, 1779, a force of 2,600 men under the command of British General William Tryon, including British regulars, Hessian mercenaries, professional German soldiers,

BURNING OF FAIRFIELD.

Burning of Fairfield, 1833

and Loyalists—Americans who sided with the crown in the Revolution—landed on the beach. Guided by George Hoyt, a Fairfield Loyalist, they marched to the town green, encountering stiff resistance from local defenders along the way.

By the time all the enemy forces had arrived at the town green, the opposition by patriot forces had grown strong enough that Tryon could not proceed toward his ultimate goal: Black Rock Harbor, and the ships he intended to burn. Tryon proceeded to set fire to several houses, as a warning of what might await those who opposed him. The patriot commander refused to be intimidated, and Tryon had several other houses torched. Still the defenders held firm.

Having burned only a small number of the homes in Fairfield, Tryon and his men headed back to their landing spot on the morning of July 8. The last enemy soldiers to leave were the German infantrymen known as Jaegers—"a banditti the vilest that was ever let loose among men," as Rev. Andrew Eliot, pastor of the First Congregational Church, described them. Before they departed, they went on a rampage, killing three civilians and, according to Rev. Eliot, setting fire "to everything that General Tryon left." The flames consumed eighty-three dwellings, fifty-five barns, twenty-eight businesses, two schools, two churches, the jail, and the courthouse. Only a few homes escaped destruction, presumably because they belonged to Loyalists.

Back on their ships, the invaders sailed off toward the Green's Farms section of town. There fourteen houses, twelve barns, and another house of worship were put to the torch.

Fairfield residents returned from nearby communities and the countryside, to which they had fled for safety before the British arrived, to find everything they had spent their lives building gone. It took nearly fifteen years before the State of Connecticut got around to compensating them for some of their losses, in the form of land grants in the wilderness of northeastern Ohio. Some people did pull up stakes and start new lives in what was called the "Firelands," after the fate that had befallen their property during Tryon's raid. However, most sold the remote land grants for a fraction of their value.

Western view of the Buckley tavern, Fairfield, ca. 1835

Gen. William Tryon made an upper room of the tavern on the Fairfield town green owned by Benjamin Buckley his command post during his 1779 raid. The building, said to date from the 1680s, was torn down about ten years after this drawing was made in 1835.

Eastern view of the Court House, Cong̲̲
and Jail in Fairfi

gational Church p 3
CT.

**Eastern view of the Court House,
Congregational church, and jail in
Fairfield, ca. 1835**

*Following Tryon's raid, the Congregational meet-
inghouse (right) on the Fairfield town green was
rebuilt on its foundation "precisely in the same
form as the one burnt, it being the wish of the
elderly people, that the house should have the same
appearance as formerly," according to nineteenth-
century historian John Warner Barber. "The same
fact is believed to be true of the form of the court
house [center] and jail [left]." The courthouse,
built in 1794, today is the Old Town Hall.*

**North view of the Academy and
Congregational church on Greenfield Hill,
Fairfield, ca. 1835**

*"This place is most justly celebrated for the prospect
which is obtained from the belfry of the church. No
other spot in Connecticut can show such a commanding, extensive, and beautiful prospect," raved Connecticut historian John Warner Barber about Greenfield
Hill in 1836. From the steeple of the Congregational
meetinghouse, built in 1760, Barber reported that the
spires of seventeen churches could be seen, including
two on Long Island, and that "in a clear day, the East
Rock near New Haven is distinctly seen." The current
Congregational church dates from 1855, but it under-
went major remodeling in the wake of a hurricane in
1944.*

North view of
on

Academy and Congregational Church
Greenfield Hill, Fairfield

Fairfield would come back. The homes, the houses of worship, the public buildings would be replaced. But it would never regain its economic energy.

Like so many of the earliest towns in Connecticut, Fairfield was whittled down geographically by the breaking away of various sections to become independent governments. In 1767 Redding was formed from Fairfield, and twenty years later Weston (which included modern Easton as well) was incorporated as a separate town. A portion of Fairfield was cut off to form the town of Westport in 1835. The Green's Farms section became part of Westport in 1853. A particularly painful blow came in 1870, when the Black Rock section, including its harbor, was appropriated by Bridgeport.

The village of Southport, on the west bank of the Mill River, grew rapidly as a trading port in the early 1800s. As of 1836, "more shipping is owned in this place in proportion to its size, than in any other place between New York and Boston," noted historian John

Pulpit on the Rock, ca. 1908–1909

Renowned Unitarian minister Rev. Samuel Osgood delivered sermons from this unusual pulpit he had constructed on Unquowa Road during the mid-1800s. Today what was Rev. Osgood's summer home, Mosswood, is the site of the Mosswood Condominiums.

Boyle's Beach Casino, ca. 1910

Boyle's Beach Casino, located across the street from cottages at Fairfield Beach, was a popular dance hall in the early twentieth century. Despite its name, gambling probably wasn't part of the entertainment.

Warner Barber. One of its best-known exports was the locally grown Southport onion, desirable in part because it stored well for long periods of time—an important quality in a crop destined for distant ports.

Even after the arrival of the railroad, which provided a mode of transportation in many ways superior to ships, the Southport onion kept the village after which it was named alive as a shipping center. During the 1890s one hundred thousand barrels of onions were being shipped from Southport each year. However, cutworms that damaged the onions and competition from growers farther west eventually spelled the end of the onion industry in Fairfield.

Fairfield wasn't swept up in the rapid industrialization that spurred phenomenal population and economic growth in coastal towns like Bridgeport, New Haven, and New London during the decades following the Civil War. It retained its rural farming character, which made it an appealing location for urbanites who wanted to build a summer home a convenient train's ride from Manhattan. Some of these "cottages" were grand mansions, including

Cottages Along the Shore, Fairfield Beach, Fairfield, Conn.

"Cottages Along the Shore, Fairfield Beach," ca. 1930s

Youngsters watch as men pitch horseshoes in the sand at the beach in front of a few of the many cottages that lined Fairfield Beach in the early twentieth century.

Hearthstone Hall and the forty-room Mailands, built in 1907, which found new lives as part of Fairfield University. People seeking a seaside getaway who couldn't afford a separate summer house rented one of the cottages that were proliferating along Fairfield's coast, lodged in resort hotels like the hundred-room Fairfield House, or made day trips to the beach.

Fairfield got its first taste of significant ethnic diversity in the 1840s and 1850s with the arrival of refugees from the Irish potato famine. By 1860 nearly one out of every eight residents was Irish.

Fairfield became the home of a small number of factories beginning around the turn of the twentieth century. Local firms were turning out everything from machine tools to rubber to underwear. Immigrants began arriving from countries including Hungary, Poland, Russia, and Sweden to take jobs in the factories. Fairfield's population grew steadily and significantly, from 3,748 in 1880 to 6,134 in 1910.

But it was the powerful ripple effect of the industrial boom in next-door neighbor Bridgeport beginning with World War I that most profoundly affected Fairfield. Tens of thousands of workers flocked to Bridgeport to labor in the plants that produced weapons for Allied troops. The city couldn't hope to house all of them.

Fairfield was the logical, convenient, and attractive place for many of these newcomers to find homes. Between 1910 and 1930 Fairfield's population nearly tripled, to 17,218. Commuter trains and the automobile turned this temporary phenomenon into a permanent pattern, with New Yorkers also finding Fairfield a convenient place from which to commute. Residential developments sprang up on what had once been farmland.

One of these transplanted Manhattanites started a major corporation right in her kitchen. Margaret Rudkin's youngest son suffered from both asthma and severe allergies that severely restricted what he could eat. Margaret proceeded to bake some all-natural, stone-ground, whole-wheat bread that, in addition to not aggravating her son's medical problems, was delicious. She called the bread "Pepperidge Farm," after the Rudkin family's Fairfield home.

Demand for Pepperidge Farm bread, still all baked in Margaret Rudkin's kitchen and a converted garage, grew by word—and taste—of mouth. By 1940 Rudkin was selling a million loaves of bread a year. She opened a bakery in Fairfield in 1940, then in 1947 established a brand new one in Norwalk, Connecticut.

The post–World War II baby boom and its related phenomenon, suburbanization, aided by construction of the Connecticut Turnpike in the 1950s, sent Fairfield's population skyrocketing. The number of residents grew from 30,489 in 1950 to 56,487 in 1970.

During the last decades of the twentieth century, many of the several dozen factories that had operated in Fairfield for generations either shut down or moved out of town. The Fairfield Rubber Company, once the town's biggest industrial employer, ceased production. The Bullard Company, maker of lathes and machine tools, closed in the early 1980s after more than seventy years in Fairfield. McKesson & Robbins, makers of cosmetics and drugs, shut its doors in 1988.

Filling some of the economic gap created by the departure of industry was the growth of higher education. Fairfield University was established in 1942, and Sacred Heart University in 1963. Today, their combined student bodies exceed ten thousand. Another major boost was the General Electric Corporation's decision to move its headquarters to Fairfield in 1974.

7

BRIDGEPORT

The title character of Mark Twain's *Connecticut Yankee in King Arthur's Court,* being guided through the landscape of sixth-century England to which he had been mysteriously transported, spotted "on a hill, a vast gray fortress, with towers and turrets."

"'Bridgeport?'" said I, pointing," the Yankee asked.

"'Camelot,'" his guide replied.

Bridgeport in the 1880s, when Mark Twain was writing his time-travel fantasy, was in its own way an industrial "Camelot"—a place of visionaries and of manufacturing marvels. Mammoth factories of stone and brick were turning out goods like lamps and guns faster than anyone had thought possible, as well as products that hadn't even been dreamed of a few decades earlier, like sewing machines.

Bridgeport's leading citizen, P. T. Barnum, had spent a long lifetime bringing before the world wonders both false, like the Feejee Mermaid, and genuine, like the perfectly formed midget Tom Thumb, who topped out at twenty-eight inches tall, that at times must have seemed conjured by magic. Barnum's first home in Bridgeport had indeed looked like a palace from some exotic, mystical past.

The area that makes up modern Bridgeport was settled by English immigrants as early as the 1640s and grew slowly for more than a century. Midway between Stratford and Fairfield, the area was allowed to form its own religious parish, Pequonnock, in 1691.

It wasn't until after the American Revolution that Bridgeport truly began to develop. Both Stratford and Fairfield built up a thriving maritime trade with ports on the Atlantic coast and the West Indies. In 1800, Bridgeport was made a borough of the town of Stratford, and in 1821 the town of Bridgeport was established. At last, the city of Bridgeport, geographically larger than the town, was incorporated in 1836.

Bridgeport, ca. 1835

Bridgeport, seen from the eastern bank of the Pequonnock River, "at this time, is rapidly increasing in wealth and population," according to historian John Warner Barber, who drew this sketch around 1835. What in 1800 had been a village of several dozen houses, and even fewer stores and sailing vessels, had become a community of more than four thousand with a thriving maritime trade, shipyards, and small firms making saddles, hats, shirts, and carriages.

The steamboat just south of the bridge had begun making a daily run to New York City in 1834. However, Bridgeport residents had their eye on even bigger things, transportation-wise. It was incorporated as a city in 1836 largely for the purpose of enabling it to issue municipal bonds for funding that would entice the Housatonic Railroad to make Bridgeport the terminus on Long Island Sound of its planned north–south line in western Connecticut.

The ploy worked. In 1840 the tracks were completed between Bridgeport and New Milford, and two years later they extended all the way to Massachusetts. The produce of interior farms now could be conveniently and quickly transported by train to Bridgeport, from whence they could be shipped to distant markets.

Construction of the Housatonic Railroad linked Bridgeport to Massachusetts by 1842, and rail connection with New York City was established in 1849. These transportation routes opened up new economic opportunities for Bridgeport and also contributed to the establishment of the city's first sizeable ethnic minority: refugees from the Irish potato famine, who arrived in such large numbers that by 1850 fully one-seventh of Bridgeport's residents had been born in Ireland.

The 1840s saw the arrival of that newcomer who would profoundly affect Bridgeport's future: Phineas Taylor Barnum. P. T. Barnum, as he is better known, was a native of nearby Bethel, Connecticut. By the time he took up residence in Bridgeport in 1846, Barnum was famous as the proprietor of the American Museum in Manhattan, where he displayed genuine curiosities like the original Siamese twins, Chang and Eng, along with outright fakes. In 1871 Barnum went into the circus business, which for a number of years had its winter quarters in Bridgeport.

IRANISTAN, THE RESIDENCE OF MR. BARNUM.   1851

Iranistan, the Residence of Mr. Barnum, 1851

The first of the four homes P. T. Barnum occupied in Bridgeport was Iranistan, which he built in 1848, three years before this illustration was produced. Barnum's fondness for the flamboyant was given free rein in Iranistan. It was modeled after the Royal Pavilion at Brighton, England, built around 1820 for King George IV, in a style featuring onion domes and minarets found in the architecture of India. Iranistan burned down in 1857.

A. L. Cheney & Co., 10 John Street, ca. 1881

Several men, presumably employees, pose in front of the 10 John Street office of A. L. Cheney & Co., publishers of the Bridgeport Weekly Eagle *newspaper, around 1881. Of even greater interest are the two figures in the doorway to the right, one of whom is probably Ying Lee, who operated a Chinese laundry at 8 John Street in the early 1880s.*

Barnum dedicated himself to the good of his adopted city. He gave the land for Seaside Park, donated money for the Barnum Museum, and contributed to many other civic causes. He energetically promoted East Bridgeport as a rising center of industry. He was mayor of Bridgeport for one year and served in the Connecticut House of Representatives.

Barnum was not alone in appreciating Bridgeport's potential. Factories small and large, producing everything from sewing machines to firearms to corsets, were established and flourished. The new jobs they created were filled largely by immigrants from an increasing variety of foreign countries. In 1890 the city's population was 48,886—a tenfold increase over what it had been just half a century earlier.

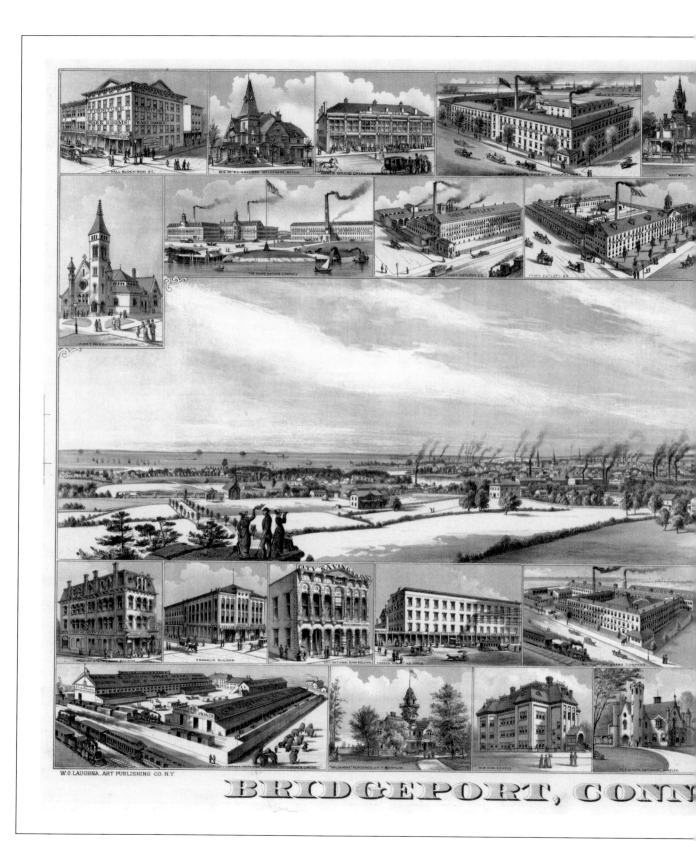

BRIDGEPORT, CONN

Bridgeport, Conn., 1882

By 1882, Bridgeport had been transformed from the thriving village of 1840 into the rapidly developing center of industry depicted in this bird's-eye view. It was home to major manufacturers that included the Bridgeport Brass Company, the Wheeler & Wilcox sewing machine factory, and the Warner Corset Company. Its population exceeded thirty thousand. And it was just the beginning.

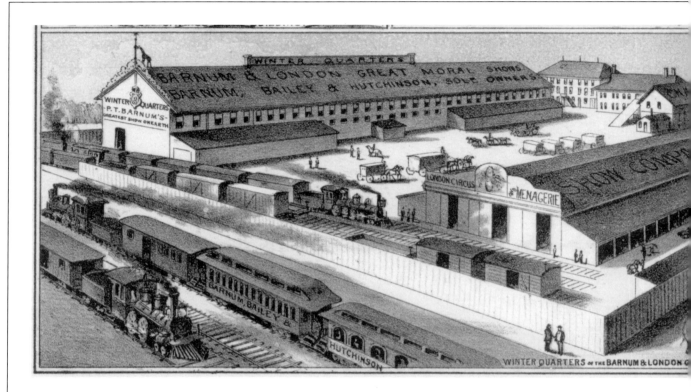

Circus in Winter Quarters, 1882.

P.T. Barnum merged his "Greatest Show on Earth" with a circus run by John Bailey in 1881. The new entertainment enterprise, elephants and all, spent the winter of 1882 in Bridgeport at headquarters depicted in a vignette from an 1882 bird's-eye view.

That astonishing growth accelerated during World War I. Of the small arms and ammunition manufactured in the United States for the Allies, two-thirds were produced in Bridgeport. That feat was made possible only by a phenomenal influx of new workers, with the result that the city's population skyrocketed from 100,000 to 150,000 in a single year.

The expansion continued after the war's end. By 1930 there were more than five hundred factories in Bridgeport, and its population had remained close to that 150,000 mark.

Baseball: Bridgeports vs. New Britains, Thursday, July 23, 1885

The "Bridgeports" who played in this game were probably the Bridgeport Giants team. The Giants ended the 1885 season, their first, with a record of twelve wins and seventeen losses.

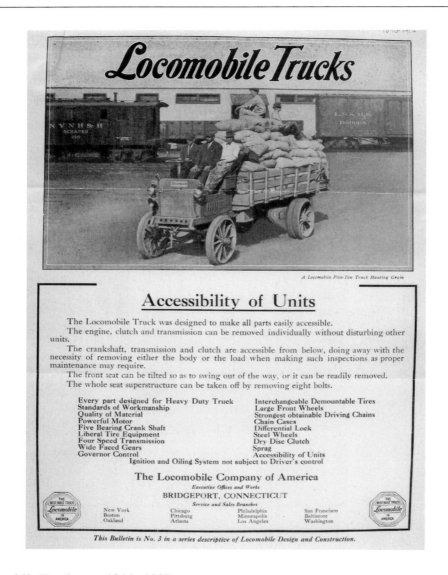

A Locomobile Five-Ton Truck Hauling Grain

Accessibility of Units

The Locomobile Truck was designed to make all parts easily accessible.

The engine, clutch and transmission can be removed individually without disturbing other units.

The crankshaft, transmission and clutch are accessible from below, doing away with the necessity of removing either the body or the load when making such inspections as proper maintenance may require.

The front seat can be tilted so as to swing out of the way, or it can be readily removed.

The whole seat superstructure can be taken off by removing eight bolts.

Every part designed for Heavy Duty Truck
Standards of Workmanship
Quality of Material
Powerful Motor
Five Bearing Crank Shaft
Liberal Tire Equipment
Four Speed Transmission
Wide Faced Gears
Governor Control

Interchangeable Demountable Tires
Large Front Wheels
Strongest obtainable Driving Chains
Chain Cases
Differential Lock
Steel Wheels
Dry Disc Clutch
Sprag
Accessibility of Units

Ignition and Oiling System not subject to Driver's control

The Locomobile Company of America

Executive Offices and Works

BRIDGEPORT, CONNECTICUT

Service and Sales Branches

New York
Boston
Oakland

Chicago
Pittsburg
Atlanta

Philadelphia
Minneapolis
Los Angeles

San Francisco
Baltimore
Washington

This Bulletin is No. 3 in a series descriptive of Locomobile Design and Construction.

Locomobile Trucks, ca. 1911–1927

The Locomobile Company of America turned out motor vehicles in Bridgeport for nearly thirty years. Founded in 1899, it manufactured primarily luxury automobiles. In contrast to the Detroit assembly lines, which produced huge numbers of cars that the average worker could afford, Locomobile emphasized costly quality in its automobiles. Each Locomobile body was assembled by several skilled employees, who in 1918 were expected to complete a maximum of four cars a day. Such craftsmanship came with a steep price tag. In 1917 a Locomobile car sold for $4,750—the equivalent of more than $76,000 in twenty-first-century dollars.

In 1911 Locomobile also began manufacturing trucks, like the one shown in this advertisement. The company went out of business in 1927, and its plant on Main Street has long since disappeared.

Bridgeport Brass Company parade float, ca. 1917

Founded in 1865, the Bridgeport Brass Company was one of the city's largest employers for nearly a century. By 1896 its 200,000-square-foot factory at Willard and Crescent Avenue employed eight hundred workers. Forty years later, that number had quadrupled to 3,250.

The bicycle lamps displayed on this parade float from around 1917 were just a few examples of goods the firm made, not just of brass, but of copper and bronze as well. Over the decades its product line included hundreds of different items, from fittings to fastenings, wire to automobile parts, lamps to shell casings for ammunition.

Aerial view of Bridgeport Harbor, ca. 1920–1927

By 1932, Bridgeport, seen during the 1920s in this aerial photograph, was, according to the Connecticut State Register and Manual, *universally recognized as "one of the greatest industrial centers in the world." Home to hundreds of manufacturing operations, its population had more than doubled since 1900.*

But from this high point Bridgeport, along with the rest of the nation, plunged into the Great Depression. The impact on Bridgeport was catastrophic. Unemployment soared to 25 percent, and the city government was overwhelmed by demands for services that broke its budget.

Bridgeport residents responded to this crisis in a startling way. In 1933 they elected a Socialist, Jasper McLevy, as mayor. McLevy was one of their own, a Bridgeport native, lifelong city resident, and labor activist. And regardless of what he called himself, McLevy proved to be an efficient and honest manager of the city's finances and operations. For the next twenty-four years, Bridgeport voters kept McLevy and a Socialist city council in office.

World War II, with its insatiable demand for weapons and other military-related goods, helped raise Bridgeport from the depths of the Depression. By 1950 its population hit its all-time peak of 158,709.

The last half of the twentieth century was an era of steady decline for industry throughout the Northeast, as factories that had served as keystones of urban economies for generations closed or moved their operations to other parts of the country or even overseas. Bridgeport was hit particularly hard by this development, losing nearly twenty thousand residents between 1950 and 2000. It remains, however, the largest city, in terms of population, in Connecticut.

8

STRATFORD

$\mathcal{L}$ ong Island Sound and its freshwater tributaries dominated the first three hundred years of Stratford's story. In the mid-twentieth century, just as the abundance of sea and streams was running dry, Stratford found its future in the skies.

Settled in 1639, Stratford quickly took advantage of the bounty of the surrounding waters. The Housatonic River teemed with salmon, sturgeon, and especially shad. By the mid-1800s, netting shad as they swam from the sea upriver to their spawning grounds was one of the most profitable lines of work the town had to offer. Some days twelve thousand shad might be pulled from the Housatonic.

Within half a century, the shad were gone from the Housatonic. The fatal blow was dealt by construction in 1869 of a dam farther up the river that prevented the fish from reaching their spawning grounds.

Salmon and sturgeon were originally plentiful in the Housatonic as well. Both these fish had disappeared from the river by the middle of the 1800s—the salmon fished out, the sturgeon killed off by pollution.

Oysters, however, were the kings of the Stratford seafood industry. An important part of the Native American diet, they continued to be so for the English settlers as well. With the advance of time, oysters were not just consumed locally, but shipped to large cities, and even to Europe.

Oystering became a less important part of Stratford's economy at the beginning of the twentieth century due to a number of factors. Less onerous jobs in manufacturing became available, and starfish were severely damaging the oyster harvest. Pollution contaminated shellfish in Long Island Sound. By the 1960s oystering had all but ceased. In recent decades, efforts to clean up Long Island Sound and to reestablish oysters have sparked a slow, sometimes fitful, comeback.

WILLIAM SAMUEL JOHNSON, L.L.D.
Third President of Columbia College
1787 to 1800.

William Samuel Johnson, L.L.D., ca. 1820

In 1787, William Samuel Johnson of Stratford was one of three men who signed the U.S. Constitution on behalf of Connecticut. Two years after that, he was one of Connecticut's first U.S. senators. These are major historical achievements, made even more remarkable by the fact that a decade earlier Johnson had been arrested on suspicion of collaborating with the enemy British in a time of war.

Johnson was an Anglican, son of Stratford's first Anglican pastor. However, Johnson's career made it clear that membership in the Church of England was not necessarily a handicap to advancement in colonial Connecticut. Johnson was a rich, Yale-educated lawyer who was elected to both houses of Connecticut's legislature and was chosen to represent Connecticut in a complex legal case in London that lasted four years.

Johnson opposed the British government's increasingly repressive treatment of its colonies in the 1760s and 1770s. But as the relationship deteriorated, Johnson could not bring himself to accept a permanent separation between the two. He refused to represent Connecticut at the First Continental Congress in Philadelphia in 1774. Once the bloody fighting erupted, he gave up his seat in the Connecticut legislature and maintained a low profile. He would not swear allegiance to the new, independent Connecticut, and as a result he was prohibited from practicing law.

Johnson's refusal to hop on the revolutionary bandwagon made him a suspicious person, particularly considering his membership in the Church of England, which acknowledged the British monarch as its earthly head. His attempt to remain uncommitted finally became untenable in the summer of 1779.

British troops commanded by Gen. William Tryon, whom Johnson knew, had raided, ransacked, and torched several coastal towns, including New Haven and Fairfield. Stratford residents, fearing it was only a matter of time before it was their turn to be attacked, asked Johnson to negotiate with Tryon to spare Stratford. A rumor began to spread that Johnson had suggested Stratford residents reject American independence in exchange for Tryon's agreement not to attack them.

When Connecticut military officials picked up on this rumor, soldiers were sent to take Johnson into custody. He was placed under house arrest in Farmington, Connecticut. He appealed to Connecticut Governor Jonathan Trumbull Sr. and his advisers, denying he had ever made such a treasonous suggestion. Johnson swore an oath of allegiance and was allowed to return to Stratford.

With the end of the Revolution in 1783, Johnson returned to politics. His efforts to remain neutral throughout the war and the disagreements leading up to it had not tarnished his reputation. He went back into state service, which was soon followed by his selection as delegate to the Constitutional Convention and election to the U.S. Senate.

S. Western view of the Episcopal church and the Academy at Stratford, Con.

Southwestern view of the Episcopal Church and the Academy at Stratford, ca. 1835

Christ Episcopal Church, the Anglican house of worship built in Stratford in 1743, was "finished in a very neat and elegant manner," according to its first pastor, with the architecture "being allowed in some things to exceed anything before done in New England"—probably a reference to the detailing, including the elegant top of its 120-foot-tall steeple, visible in this 1835 drawing. The church stood for another twenty-three years, when it was replaced by the current building.

Building vessels to sail the seas was also important in Stratford's early economy. Ships were being built as early as the 1600s in yards where Ferry Creek joins the Housatonic River. Stratford men also served as commanders and crews on ships that fought to secure independence from Great Britain in the American Revolution, then to retain it during the War of 1812.

Early in the eighteenth century Stratford was the beachhead in Connecticut for a religious minority: Anglicans, as members of the Church of England were called. At that time fewer than one hundred Anglicans could be found among Connecticut's thirty-five thousand people. The rest of the colony's population belonged to the Congregational church, which was the established, government-supported religion of Connecticut.

Most of the colony's tiny Anglican minority resided in Stratford. In 1706 a representative of the Church of England arrived in town to establish an Anglican church. The clergy and residents of Stratford and nearby towns "were alarmed at his coming, and took pains to prevent their neighbors and families from hearing him," according to an early Connecticut historian. This fear and hostility arose from the fact that Connecticut's Puritan settlers had originally belonged to the Church of England but had concluded that it had become corrupted by elaborate practices and customs. The Puritans had left England to

Along the Housatonic, Stratford, October 11, 1898

This landscape of a house and plain barns and outbuildings along the undeveloped banks of the Housatonic River in October 1898 reflects one local historian's recollections that Stratford, with only 3,700 people, then "was still rural in character, and her people chiefly engaged in agricultural pursuits rather than manufacturing. No automobiles, no telephones, no electric lights or street cars marred her beauty or disturbed the peaceful quiet of her elm-shaded streets."

Robert Brandt in eighteenth-century costume, ca. 1900

Why Stratford resident Robert Brandt donned this eighteenth-century garb early in the twentieth century remains a mystery. Perhaps he was taking part in a historical pageant or posing for a novelty period photograph, as the painted architectural background suggests. His luxurious mustache, however, was unlikely to have graced the face of any American in the 1700s.

Brandt was a native of Germany who came to the United States in 1857 at the age of two. By 1910 he was living in Stratford, had become an American citizen, and was employed as a wood engraver.

Igor Sikorsky and the first successful helicopter built in America, ca. 1940

Inventor and aviation pioneer Igor Sikorsky himself pilots his prototype VS-300 helicopter in this photograph, taken around 1940. The initial flight of the VS-300, described as the "world's first practical single main rotor helicopter," had taken place on September 14 of the previous year, with Sikorsky at the helm.

Sikorsky was already a successful and prosperous innovator and manufacturer of airplanes when he left his native Russia in the wake of the Bolshevik Revolution of 1917. Within a few short years he had arrived in the United States and started an airplane factory in Bridgeport, Connecticut.

While still living in Russia, Sikorsky had dedicated much time and thought toward the development of an aircraft that could take off vertically. Others in Europe were pursuing the same idea, and there had been some limited success. But the helicopter as a practical flying machine remained unrealized. Sikorsky took up the challenge again in the 1930s, and the result was the VS-300—and aviation history.

establish in North America their "purified" version of the Church of England—which the Anglicans now were looking to infiltrate.

Despite strong opposition, an Anglican congregation was formed in Stratford in 1707—the first in Connecticut. They built a church in the center of Stratford in 1743.

Stratford was reduced in size geographically by perhaps half when the modern towns of Shelton and Monroe were separated from it in 1789. It was cut in half yet again in 1797, when the northwestern section was incorporated as the new town of Trumbull.

In 1821 it was shaved down to its present size when part was taken to be included in the new town of Bridgeport.

During the early decades of the twentieth century, Stratford grew dramatically, with the arrival of manufacturing companies that would be important employers for generations to come, like the Contract Plating Company and Raybestos. In addition, establishment of a trolley line made it possible for people to commute from homes in Stratford to jobs in Bridgeport's burgeoning factories.

In 1929 the Sikorsky Aero Engineering Corporation moved into town from Bridgeport, and Stratford would never be the same. The company had been manufacturing airplanes since its founding in 1923. Production of the helicopters that had been fine-tuned to practicality by the company's owner, Igor Sikorsky, began in 1940. The demand for these new flying machines was immediate and intense: By the end of World War II, Sikorsky had built four hundred helicopters for the U.S. Army. Eight decades later, Sikorsky is the world's oldest helicopter manufacturer, a major producer of helicopters for military and civilian use, and Stratford's largest employer.

The American Shakespeare Festival was established in Stratford in 1955, and for nearly thirty years it performed the works of the immortal Bard and other playwrights in a specially constructed venue, the 1,100-seat Stratford Festival Theatre, on the banks of the Housatonic River. Among the gifted thespians who played there were Katharine Hepburn, Paul Newman, Jessica Tandy, and James Earl Jones. The theater did not prove successful financially and closed in 1982. So far, attempts to revive it have not been successful.

9.

MILFORD

*M*ilford was one of the first English settlements in Connecticut—but the approximately two hundred original Puritan migrants were not Milford's first residents. Four communities of Native Americans had been living there for generations before the English arrived in 1639, and their presence literally shaped the development of the newcomers' settlement.

The English took possession of the land from the Native Americans via a series of transactions that began in 1639 and continued into the early 1700s. Relations between the two peoples proved to be so tense that, shortly after arriving, the English surrounded their settlement with a palisade—a defensive stockade of twelve-foot-tall sharpened stakes. The irregularly shaped fortification embraced an expanse of land nearly a mile square on both banks of the Wepawaug River and contained more than sixty home lots.

The two peoples lived in uneasy proximity for more than half a century, managing to avoid a major confrontation. Early in the eighteenth century, the Native Americans began leaving Milford to live with other tribes in Connecticut and even the Six Nations on the western frontier. By the mid-1700s their number had dwindled to a few.

Milford's English settlers displayed an independent streak from the start. They operated for their first five years as a self-governing theocracy before joining the New Haven Colony, a confederation of shoreline towns, in 1644.

In 1661, two signers of the death warrant that authorized the beheading of King Charles I of England arrived in Milford. They were fleeing agents sent to track them down by the executed monarch's son, who had ascended to his father's throne. At great personal and political risk, several Milford residents hid the fugitives for two years.

For more than twenty years the New Haven Colony, of which Milford was a part, coexisted more or less peacefully with the Connecticut Colony, its larger, more powerful

Capt. S. Stow House, ca. 1910

On the frigid, foggy first night of 1777, approximately two hundred malnourished men wearing filthy rags materialized on the Milford shore. They were American soldiers who had been released after spending months as prisoners of war of the British in New York. Smallpox had broken out on the British ship transporting them home, and the panicked crew dumped the sick prisoners ashore at Milford.

Smallpox was highly contagious and untreatable. It killed one out of every six victims and left many survivors disfigured, blind, or disabled. Those who contracted the disease and survived were immune to it for life. The eighteenth century's one method of dealing with the disease was inoculation, the risky practice of deliberately infecting a person, which usually, but not always, resulted in a much milder case of smallpox than one contracted naturally.

Anyone lacking immunity who came into contact with an infected individual was courting death. Capt. Stephen Stow, who lived in this house with his wife and seven children, did just that in order to help the wretched men cast ashore that winter night.

Captain Stow, fifty, contracted smallpox during his mission of mercy. On January 27, 1777, "weak of Body but of Sound Mind and Memory," he dictated his will. Stephen Stow, henceforth known as the "martyr," died twelve days later.

Forty-six of the prisoners died and were interred in a common grave. A monument bearing the soldiers' names was erected in the Milford Cemetery in 1852, and Captain Stow's name was added twenty years later. Captain Stow's home, which dates from around 1700 and is thought to be the oldest surviving house in Milford, today is part of the Milford Historical Society's Wharf Lane complex.

neighbor to the north. Then in 1662 news arrived that a charter of government granted by King Charles II of England to the Connecticut Colony included the New Haven Colony within the Connecticut Colony boundaries. New Haven Colony officials resisted being abolished by a stroke of the royal pen. Milford leaders, however, eventually broke away on their own and joined Connecticut in 1664. A year later, the rest of the New Haven Colony surrendered to the inevitable.

A band of New Haven Colony residents were so unhappy about the takeover by Connecticut that they left for New Jersey, where they settled what would become Newark.

South view of the Congregational Churches in Milford, Ct., ca. 1835

After more than a century of existence, disagreement over issues of faith split Milford's Congregational church. In 1741, seventy members formed their own congregation, known as the Second or Plymouth Church. They built their own house of worship on the opposite side of the Wepawaug River just a few dozen feet from the First Church's meetinghouse.

By 1835 both congregations had handsome new buildings. The First Church (on the left) had been built in 1824, and the Plymouth Church in 1834.

In 1926 the two congregations reunited, healing the 185-year-old spiritual and geographical split. Today the reconstituted congregation worships in the 1824 meetinghouse.

Memorial Bridge with waterfall, ca. 1910

For the 250th anniversary of Milford's settlement in 1889, townspeople decided that "a substantial mark should be made in honor of the Founders," one that "should unite utility with the picturesque and at the same time be typical of the men and time of settlement." The result was a new stone bridge, built of granite from Leete's Island Quarry in Guilford at a cost of $3,000. It spans the Wepawaug River "upon whose banks their first habitations were placed."

Each of Milford's founders is commemorated on a separate stone in the bridge, paid for by descendants. The stone doorstep from the home of Milford native Governor Jonathan Law was incorporated into the structure.

"Picturesque" trumped "typical of the . . . time of the settlement" with the construction of "a forty foot turret tower topped with red Spanish tiles" at the southwestern end of the bridge. Carvings and fixtures on the tower acknowledge the town's original Native American inhabitants.

The dissenters included Robert Treat of Milford, who spent several years in New Jersey government before returning home in 1673 to become a key player in events that shaped the future of all New England.

Treat commanded Connecticut troops in some of the bloodiest fighting of the conflict between Native Americans and English in New England, known as King Philip's War, in 1675–1676. The English emerged the victors in the conflict, which ended Native American power in New England.

A freshly minted war hero, Treat became deputy governor of Connecticut in 1676. When the governor, William Leete, died in 1683, Treat succeeded to the top job. During his tenure, which lasted until 1698, he dealt with a threat to the Connecticut Colony's very existence.

In 1687 King James II of England tried to revoke Connecticut's Royal Charter of 1662. That document had granted Connecticut a degree of self-government that made it all but independent of English control. Connecticut officials evaded complying with orders to return the document, until finally a royal representative, backed by seventy mounted soldiers, arrived in the capital of Hartford to seize it.

In a meeting with the king's messenger, Governor Treat led Connecticut officials in a filibuster that lasted until darkness fell. According to legend, the candles illuminating the room were somehow snuffed out, and in the ensuing blackness the charter was snatched up and carried off to be hidden in a tree that became known as the Charter Oak.

During the American Revolution, Milford, like most of the Connecticut coast, suffered sporadic raids launched from British-held Long Island. One party of about three dozen British was routed by townspeople alerted by a housewife on horseback who beat the alarm on a copper kettle.

The threat to Milford led to the establishment of Fort Trumbull, a defensive fortification equipped with six cannon. The town was spared devastating British assaults like those that destroyed much of Fairfield and Norwalk.

For several decades following the American Revolution, Milford experienced a surge in shipbuilding and maritime trade. During the same time the town shrank geographically: The town of Woodbridge was incorporated from Milford in 1784, and the northern and eastern sections of Milford became the town of Orange in 1822. (West Haven was created out of Orange in 1921.) In 1832 the town of Bethany was created out of Milford.

Broad Street, ca. 1910

The transportation revolution sweeping the nation at the dawn of the twentieth century is evident in this photograph of Broad Street around 1910. A horse-drawn wagon sits next to a bicycle, an innovative vehicle first manufactured in the United States in Connecticut in 1878, and another wagon shares the road with an even more recent invention, the automobile.

Speeding cars were a problem in Milford by the time this photograph was taken. On a single day in 1906, ten motorists were nabbed for exceeding the fifteen-mile-per-hour speed limit.

During the nineteenth century, an assortment of industries, including the manufacture of carriages and shoes, flourished in Milford. Production of straw hats began before the Civil War and endured until after World War I. The oyster industry, in existence since before the Revolution, also took off in the mid-1800s. By 1940 Milford was harvesting as many as two million bushels of oysters a year. Oystering has experienced dramatic fluctuations due to pollution and disease, but it continues to be an active enterprise in Milford.

Producing seeds for sale was under way in Milford by 1840. It became a burgeoning industry with a national market following the Civil War and into the latter half of the twentieth century.

Milford celebrated its 250th anniversary in 1889 with great fanfare. Although its population had increased approximately 50 percent in the half century since 1840, it was still a relatively small town. As residents looked backward, they were unknowingly poised on the edge of a new era that would see the character of Milford's economy, population, and landscape change more in the next fifty years than they had in the previous 250.

Immigrants from more than a dozen European countries, from Sweden to Poland to Italy, caused Milford's population to more than quadruple by 1940, so much so that only roughly a third of the town's 16,439 year-round residents had both parents born in the United States. The remaining two-thirds were immigrants or the children of immigrants.

The early twentieth century saw the addition of a number of small manufacturing enterprises to Milford's economy, producing everything from locks to earmuffs. However, unlike nearby towns like Bridgeport and New Haven, which were transformed into urban giants by huge industrial enterprises, Milford remained remarkably rural. On the eve of World War II, more than a third of all the land in town was still being cultivated. The majority of farmers were recent immigrants—primarily Polish, Italian, and German—or their children.

The turn of the twentieth century brought another type of development that would significantly change Milford. With the arrival of trolley service to New Haven and Bridgeport in the 1890s, the town's beaches were easily accessible. Summer cottages began to go up on and near the shore, as did resort hotels. The advent of the automobile increased the number of summer pilgrims, and supplying the wants and needs of these visitors became a new line of business.

After World War II, several simultaneous developments accelerated the suburbanization begun decades earlier with the construction of houses for employees of factories in

The "Serial Polygamist" Governor

One of Milford's high schools is named for town native Jonathan Law, governor of the Connecticut Colony from 1741 until 1750. Law had been deputy governor for seventeen years when the death of governor Joseph Talcott elevated him to the leadership post. Law was repeatedly reelected governor until he himself died in office.

Governor Law had five wives—not simultaneously, but in succession, a practice that has been jokingly termed "serial polygamy." Marrying more than once was not unusual for men or women in the colonial period, however. Odds of dying young were much greater than today, and making a living, raising a family, and running a household were more than a widow or widower could handle alone. Still, five spouses was an extraordinary count—although not a record.

Law first married in 1698. His wife died five years later. Law remarried in 1705, but wife number two died ten months later. Nine months after her death, Law took his third wife, who lasted for eighteen years. Two years after her death, in 1726, he married his fourth wife, who died seven months later. Finally, in 1730, Law, now fifty-six years old, wed a twenty-nine-year-old woman who outlived him. By his five wives Law fathered an even dozen children—a large, but not extraordinary, number of offspring for the era.

St. Gabriel's Catholic Church, Walnut and Myrtle Beaches, Milford, Conn.

St. Gabriel's Roman Catholic Church, ca. 1940

Irish immigrants who arrived in the late 1840s to work on building the New York and New Haven Railroad were Milford's first Roman Catholic residents, and the town's first Roman Catholic church was erected in 1853. Milford's Roman Catholic population grew rapidly with the arrival of waves of Italian and Polish immigrants at the turn of the twentieth century.

 In 1908 St. Gabriel Mission was established at Wildemere Beach to serve the religious needs of the fast-growing community of summer visitors. The mission built its own chapel in 1910, and when that building went up in flames in 1923, the current St. Gabriel's Church was constructed, in the style of a Spanish mission chapel. In 1946 St. Gabriel's became an independent parish.

Bridgeport and New Haven. The portion of the Connecticut Turnpike, modern Interstate 95, through Milford was completed by 1960, making access to and from town faster and more convenient. The next two decades saw the construction of the Connecticut Post Mall and the commercial development of the Post Road. Milford's population tripled from its 16,439 in 1940 to 50,858 in 1970, about where it has remained ever since.

During the second half of the twentieth century, Milford's economy was dominated by the pen and the blade. These were the products of two new corporate citizens with the rhyming names of BIC and Schick.

In 1949, in his native France, Marcel Bich invented an improved and inexpensive ballpoint pen, with a transparent plastic barrel and a simple nonretractable point. He christened his new pen BIC, derived from his own name.

Bich entered the American market by purchasing the Waterman Pen Company in Seymour, Connecticut. Waterman was the world's major producer of fountain pens—which were rapidly being surpassed by ballpoints. In 1958 Marcel Bich moved the headquarters of the Waterman-BIC Pen Corporation (soon to be simply the BIC Corporation) to Milford.

Three years later, the Schick Safety Razor Company moved its manufacturing operations to Milford. This company, too, was named for its founder, Jacob Schick, who applied the principles of a repeating rifle to invent in 1921 a razor with blades stored in its handle. A shaver could replace a dull blade with a fresh one fed into place from the handle, eliminating the risk of cutting a hand in the process.

10.

WEST HAVEN

*W*est Haven is the state's newest town—even though its first English settlers arrived in 1648. That seeming contradiction arises from the manner in which Connecticut communities over the course of centuries sometimes split, then formed new combinations that might split again, like a confused amoeba.

West Haven started out as part of New Haven, which had been settled a decade before West Haven's first English inhabitants showed up. In 1719 it was set off as a separate religious parish, thereafter known as West Haven, but it remained part of the town of New Haven.

In 1822 West Haven separated from New Haven, not to become an independent town, but to be combined with a section taken from Milford to create an entirely new town called Orange. West Haven took a step toward autonomy when it became a borough of Orange in 1873, but it was not until 1921 that West Haven was incorporated as a completely independent town—Connecticut's 169th and last.

Shipbuilding was an important livelihood for generations of West Haven residents. It reached its peak during the construction of schooners in the 1880s, then quickly disappeared before the end of the nineteenth century as steam vessels replaced those powered by wind.

West Haven was home to several private academies during the nineteenth century, and several industries also operated during that period. One in particular, the West Haven Buckle Company, was to have a profound impact on the town's development and character, not because of what it produced, but because of a man who came to be employed there. George Kelsey moved from Middletown to West Haven in 1855, to work at the West Haven Buckle Company. By 1870 he was a wealthy buckle manufacturer who owned $60,000 in real estate and $55,000 in personal possessions.

The Green, West Haven, Conn.

The Green, ca. 1910

The West Haven town green, so serene in this postcard view from the turn of the twentieth century, was a scene of turmoil on July 5, 1779. Early that fateful morning, 1,500 British soldiers had come ashore near Savin Rock and proceeded to the green, looting along the way. After lounging on the green for a couple hours, eating food pilfered from local homes, the invaders resumed marching toward their goal of New Haven.

The redcoats had barely gotten off the green before they ran into unexpected gunfire from local patriots. An even uglier surprise awaited them as they approached the bridge over the West River: a hastily assembled band of defenders that included several dozen Yale students. The patriots moved out to engage the British, forcing them to briefly retreat. Heavily outnumbered and faced with the possibility of being surrounded by the enemy, the patriots then beat their own retreat, scurrying back across the bridge, which they proceeded to dismantle, forcing the British to take a much longer way into New Haven.

By that time Kelsey was also part owner of the West Haven Horsecar Line, which included a line to Savin Rock on the shoreline. Perceiving an opportunity, Kelsey constructed a pier more than a quarter mile long extending out from Beach Street, along with the Seaview Hotel on Savin Rock, both easily accessible via his horsecar line. It was the beginning of the ultimately massive Savin Rock Amusement Park, which entertained generations of Connecticut youngsters and grown-ups alike for nearly a century.

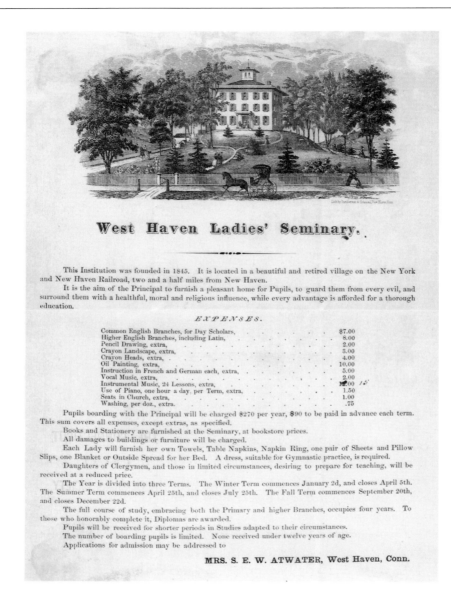

West Haven Ladies' Seminary.

This Institution was founded in 1845. It is located in a beautiful and retired village on the New York and New Haven Railroad, two and a half miles from New Haven.

It is the aim of the Principal to furnish a pleasant home for Pupils, to guard them from every evil, and surround them with a healthful, moral and religious influence, while every advantage is afforded for a thorough education.

EXPENSES.

Common English Branches, for Day Scholars,	$7.00
Higher English Branches, including Latin,	8.00
Pencil Drawing, extra,	2.00
Crayon Landscape, extra,	3.00
Crayon Heads, extra,	4.00
Oil Painting, extra,	10.00
Instruction in French and German each, extra,	5.00
Vocal Music, extra,	2.00
Instrumental Music, 24 Lessons, extra,	12.00
Use of Piano, one hour a day, per Term, extra,	1.50
Seats in Church, extra,	1.00
Washing, per doz., extra,	.75

Pupils boarding with the Principal will be charged $270 per year, $90 to be paid in advance each term. This sum covers all expenses, except extras, as specified.

Books and Stationery are furnished at the Seminary, at bookstore prices.

All damages to buildings or furniture will be charged.

Each Lady will furnish her own Towels, Table Napkins, Napkin Ring, one pair of Sheets and Pillow Slips, one Blanket or Outside Spread for her Bed. A dress, suitable for Gymnastic practice, is required.

Daughters of Clergymen, and those in limited circumstances, desiring to prepare for teaching, will be received at a reduced price.

The Year is divided into three Terms. The Winter Term commences January 2d, and closes April 5th. The Summer Term commences April 25th, and closes July 25th. The Fall Term commences September 20th, and closes December 22d.

The full course of study, embracing both the Primary and higher Branches, occupies four years. To those who honorably complete it, Diplomas are awarded.

Pupils will be received for shorter periods in Studies adapted to their circumstances.

The number of boarding pupils is limited. None received under twelve years of age.

Applications for admission may be addressed to

MRS. S. E. W. ATWATER, West Haven, Conn.

West Haven Ladies' Seminary, ca. 1857–1875

The West Haven Ladies' Seminary, later known as the Oak Hill Ladies' Seminary, operated in West Haven for more than three decades before and after the Civil War. In the 1870s, the student body numbered around seventy girls, some from as far away as California, Colorado, Alabama, and Missouri.

The school was pricey: The $270 fee quoted for boarding students would be the equivalent of more than $4,000 today—and that was before adding any of the extras. The school's curriculum included English, foreign languages, art, and music, but not science, mathematics, geography, or history, as some other female academies offered. That suggests that the school's goal was to prepare young women for lives as conventional, cultured wives, rather than for self-supporting occupations.

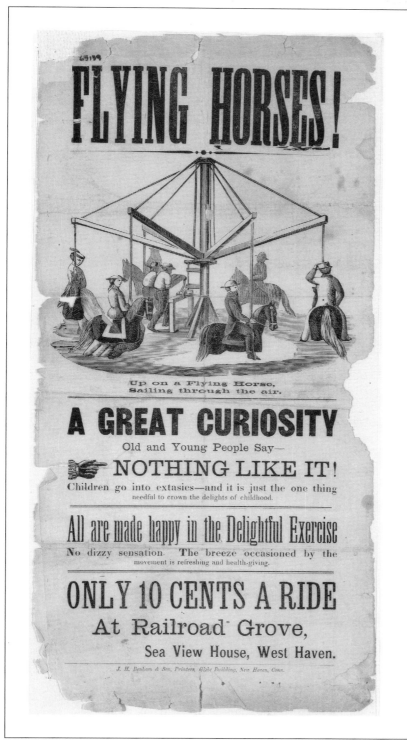

*Up on a Flying Horse,
Sailing through the air.*

*Flying Horses!, ca.
1875*

*A ride on this manually
powered carousel, the forerunner of the more familiar
mechanized merry-go-
round, promised happiness
and health to young and
old alike willing to part
with a dime. The contrap-
tion was called "Flying
Horses" because the men
working the crank would
get it whirling fast enough
for centrifugal force to
push the horses out away
from the center, creating
the sensation of flight.*

*The ride was located
at the Sea View House,
which was built on Savin
Rock in West Haven at the
beginning of the 1870s.
Within a few years Savin
Rock would develop into
a wonderland of thrill-
ing, enchanting rides
that would make the Fly-
ing Horses seem tame by
comparison.*

The Pebble of Oyster River, ca. 1900–1940

This enterprising quartet peddled postcards, souvenirs, and clams probably gathered with the tools held by the three men in the foreground, and also rented boats, out of a makeshift store on the Oyster River, which can be seen in the background.

Savin Rock's heyday came during the 1920s. In the subsequent decades an array of forces, from nature to changes in the patterns of life, conspired to send the park on a slow but inexorable slide to extinction.

In some ways Savin Rock was a victim of its own success. For years it expanded physically, but eventually there was simply no more space available to grow. The crowds overwhelmed the almost nonexistent sanitary facilities.

The Great Depression of the 1930s left many people with little money for amusements, cutting into Savin Rock's attendance. Long Island Sound became increasingly polluted. Hurricanes in 1938 and 1955 ravaged the park's waterfront facilities.

With the proliferation of the automobile, people opted to drive to places rather than take public transportation. This led to the decline and eventual disappearance of the trolleys and ferries that once served Savin Rock. At the same time, it wasn't possible to create sufficient parking for the cars of people driving to the park, which also created enormous traffic jams on roads leading into it. At last, in 1967, Savin Rock fell before bulldozers in the name of urban renewal.

West Haven's economy took new turns during the last half of the twentieth century. In 1968 a subsidiary of Miles Laboratories opened in town. Known since 1980 as Bayer Pharmaceuticals, the firm grew into West Haven's largest employer and taxpayer before closing its West Haven plant in 2006. In 1960 New Haven College moved into the New Haven County Orphanage, and it has since grown into the University of New Haven, with more than 2,400 undergraduates as well as graduate students.

RECREATION

During the nineteenth century there emerged a middle class of Americans whose jobs in factories and offices allowed them leisure time to pursue activities purely for relaxation and enjoyment. This phenomenon, combined with the advent of various methods of convenient, quick, and affordable transportation, including steamboats, trains, trolleys, and, at the very end of the century, automobiles, spurred the development of a new industry along Connecticut's Long Island Sound shoreline.

The beaches, the water, and the unspoiled landscapes drew city residents looking for respite from the clamor and grit and hustle of life in the burgeoning metropolises. Hotels and cottages were constructed to house these hordes of vacationers; restaurants opened to feed them; stores expanded to provide supplies for those occupying or renting a summer home for an extended stay. And a new creation, the amusement park, was invented to provide thrills like none experienced ever before.

The Beach

Going to the beach has changed dramatically since the post–Civil War era. Most obviously from the images here, the bathing suits got progressively skimpier and the beaches increasingly crowded.

Beach at Westbrook, ca. 1872. One of the first beach resorts along the Connecticut coast was in Westbrook. Judging from this photograph from the early 1870s, proper beach attire was no different from what one would wear on a city street. A couple of youngsters appear to have ventured into Long Island Sound, but the fully clothed grown-ups have remained high and dry.

Some of these conservative beachgoers likely arrived in the horse-drawn carriage driven down the ruts that appear to be the closest thing to a road. Other possibilities are the sailboat, rowboat, or canoe pulled up onto the beach.

Steele and Annis family members in bathing costumes, Westbrook, 1889. By 1889, men, women, and children all had taken the plunge into the Sound at Westbrook—at least up to their knees. For their July water venture, all eight members of the Steele and Annis families were wearing garments that appear to be specifically designed for going into the water—although most were still covered from neck to knee.

Hammonasset Beach State Park

Hammonasset Beach State Park, Madison, 1960s. By the 1960s the sun, sand, salt water—and sometimes surf—attracted throngs to shoreline beaches like Hammonasset Beach State Park in Madison. Both men's and women's bathing suits bared far more skin than the beachgoers of the nineteenth century could ever have imagined. By this time major amenities were provided, including a broad wooden boardwalk, benches, trash cans, and lights.

The Ark, Indian Neck, Branford, 1908. Frolicking at the beach worked up hearty appetites that could be sated at refreshment stands like the Ark at Indian Neck in Branford.

Places to Stay

As increasing numbers of people sought out the delights of Connecticut's coastline, hotels by the dozens and cottages by the thousands sprang up to accommodate them.

Sachem's Head Hotel, Guilford, 1860, detail. Even before the Civil War, portions of Connecticut's coast had become popular destinations for prosperous vacationers from New York. The Sachem's Head Hotel in Guilford was only a three-and-a-half-hour trip by train from Manhattan.

The Sachem's Head had been expanded and enhanced for the summer of 1860. In addition to the pleasures of nearby Long Island Sound, the establishment's four hundred guests could choose among an array of activities, including billiards, bowling, fishing, partying aboard a yacht, and sailing. Astonishingly—and incredibly—this broadside assures prospective visitors that "mosquitoes are never seen at the Head."

SACHEM'S HEAD HOTEL,
GUILFORD, CONN.

The proprietor of this well-known first class fashionable Summer-House would inform its former patrons and the public generally, that he has built on three hundred feet this spring, making seventy-four new bed rooms, new dining room forty by one hundred, new parlor forty by seventy. Every room in the house is newly furnished with *new Carpets* and new Cottage Furniture. The Hotel is of modern construction, built on an extensive scale, with accommodations for four hundred guests; beautifully located on Long Island Sound, fourteen miles east of New Haven, on the New London and Stonington Railroad; new Billiard Room, with three new tables, two new ten pin alleys at a convenient distance from the house, and twelve new Bathing Houses. Fishing is not surpassed on the Sound. A new yacht of forty-five tons, and several small sail boats, will be constantly on hand, ready for parties.

Going from New York to Sachem's Head, take the 8 A. M. train and 3 P. M. train; *check and ticket* to Sachem's Head direct, changing cars at New Haven—time through 3½ hours. From New Haven to the Head at 7½ A. M., 11 A. M. and 6 P. M.—time forty minutes. At the Sachem's Head depot will be found one of Cook's best four horse Omnibuses, new and clean, to carry you direct to the House.

A new Barn, one hundred by fifty-two feet, has been built this spring, which will accommodate fifty horses. Eight acres of land have been enclosed and filled with ornamental and fruit trees, walks, &c.

The House will be opened for the reception of company on the 20th day of June next, under the immediate superintendence of the owner.

N. B. Mosquitoes are never seen at the Head.

Montowese House, Indian Neck, Branford, ca. 1908. Guests of the Montowese House at Branford's Indian Neck, shown around 1908, included Mark Twain.

Griswold Hotel/House, Eastern Point, Groton, ca. 1920–1939. The Griswold Hotel/House on Eastern Point in Groton was a massive five-story, four-hundred-room hotel. It was built in 1906 by Morton Plant, who constructed a lavish mansion nearby to serve as his summer home. The Griswold Houses was torn down in 1968.

Cottages at White Beach, East Lyme, ca. 1880–1899. Cottages like these at White Beach in East Lyme, sprang up by the thousands all along the shoreline.

Sleepy Hollow Cabins

BRANFORD, CONN.

Sleepy Hollow Cabins, Branford, 1954. Those of modest means could still enjoy a getaway to the shoreline by staying at accommodations like the Sleepy Hollow Cabins in Branford.

Amusement Parks

There were several amusement parks along the Connecticut coast, but West Haven's Savin Rock reigned supreme. It started with the Sea View Hotel, built in the late 1800s by George Kelsey, an entrepreneur who expanded the entertainment available to his guests to include a zoo, a museum, and a dance hall.

In the 1870s "rides" began to appear, at first powered by people or animals, later by electricity. Trolleys and ferries brought thousands of folks looking for a day of carefree entertainment to the rapidly expanding park.

Savin Rock Amusement Park's heyday occurred during the 1920s. There were roller coasters, carousels, water rides, boxing matches, stage shows, live entertainment, restaurants, funhouses, games of chance—and much, much more.

Savin Rock went into a slow decline around the time of the Great Depression of the 1930s. It held on until the late 1960s, when the aging and now-passé park fell before the bulldozers of urban renewal.

The Midway, Savin Rock, Conn.

The Midway, Savin Rock, West Haven, ca. 1930s. The midway was popular with visitors eager to try their luck at a variety of games of chance. Raids on some of the games by the state police were not unknown.

"THE DEVIL," SAVIN ROCK, CONN.

"The Devil," Savin Rock, West Haven, ca. 1925–1932. The Devil roller coaster on Liberty Pier carried thrill-seeking riders right out over the water. The Devil went up in flames in 1932, just seven years after it opened.

2971—Chute the Chutes, White City, New Haven, Conn.

"Chute the Chutes," Savin Rock, West Haven, ca. 1901–1907. Chute the Chutes plunged riders in boats down an incline into a two-hundred-foot-long pool. The attraction opened in 1903 and burned down a mere nine years later.

WILCOX PAVILLION, SAVIN ROCK, NEW HAVEN, CT

YALE STUDIO, Savin Rock, Conn.

Mr. and Mrs. Marshall Brown, Albert M. Butler, and friend Irene E. Chinn, August 1908. A photograph was a popular souvenir of an outing at Savin Rock. The couples in this image, identified on the back as Mr. and Mrs. Marshall Brown, Albert M. Butler, and Irene E. Chinn were probably from Norwich, Connecticut.

Fun for All Ages

Ringling Brothers Circus parade, New Haven, 1907. The lure of the exotic and the unusual drew the attention of New Haven residents of all ages to the Ringling Brothers Circus parade in 1907.

The Midway, Roton Point, South Norwalk, Conn.

The Midway, Roton Point, South Norwalk, Conn., ca. 1910. Roton Point was a popular amusement park in South Norwalk from the late 1880s until the beginning of World War II.

Sailboat at Mulberry Point, Guilford, ca. 1910–1929. The waters off Guilford's Mulberry Point offered delightful sailing in the early decades of the twentieth century.

11

NEW HAVEN

A band of English Puritans, led by the Reverend John Davenport, settled New Haven in 1638. Their first stop in the New World had been Boston, but, finding the government there too religiously liberal for their tastes, they moved on to establish their own community. In New Haven, only members of the church were allowed to vote. The government, based strictly on the Bible, didn't include any features that were not found in holy scripture, such as trial by jury.

Over the next twenty-five years the settlement at New Haven became the center of the New Haven Colony—an entity entirely separate from the Connecticut Colony, which was centered around the Connecticut River towns of Hartford, Windsor, and Wethersfield. Some New Haven residents went forth to start new settlements along the coast, such as Guilford, while other towns established independently, like Branford, subsequently joined the colony.

By 1662, the New Haven Colony included New Haven, Guilford, Branford, Milford, and Stamford. That year King Charles II of England signed what amounted to a death warrant for the colony: a royal charter of government for the Connecticut Colony that included within its boundaries all of the New Haven Colony.

Many New Haven Colony leaders and residents fiercely objected to being absorbed into the Connecticut Colony, which they also considered insufficiently strict concerning religious issues. However, resistance proved futile, and in 1665 the New Haven Colony became part of the Connecticut Colony.

In 1701 the Connecticut General Assembly made New Haven co-capital of Connecticut with Hartford. From then on the assembly held its May session in Hartford and its October session in New Haven. The assembly didn't go on record as to why it made this fundamental change in the colonial government.

A Plan of the Town of New Haven. With all the buildings in 1748

A map of New Haven in 1748 depicts the grid of nine squares, with the green at the center, set out when New Haven was settled in 1638 and maintained down to the present day. The green was a much different place from the well-maintained grassy open space it is today. Several buildings stood on it, including the Congregational meetinghouse, a school, and the state house. Yale College's first—and still only—building stood across College Street from the green. Also, much of the green was being used, as it had been since 1639, as a graveyard, as indicated by the crudely sketched tombstones and table stones.

Yale College, which had been operating in a series of temporary locations since its founding in 1701, settled permanently in New Haven in 1716. In 1755 another cultural landmark occurred in New Haven: publication of the first newspaper ever issued in Connecticut. Titled the *Connecticut Gazette,* it consisted of four pages printed once a week.

New Haven's harbor wasn't deep enough to accommodate large sailing vessels, but significant maritime trade with the West Indies and towns along the Atlantic coast did

PL. III.

YALE COLLEGE.

J.W.Barber del.et.Sc.

Yale College, 1825

By 1825 Yale's original wooden structure had been replaced by a row of brick buildings, including a chapel, library, chemical laboratory, and "mineralogical cabinet." A group of young men, presumably students, are depicted engaged in some kind of ball game on the fenced-in green across from the college.

develop, beginning in the mid-1700s. One of the many men involved in this commerce was a merchant named Benedict Arnold, who arrived in New Haven from his native Norwich in 1762.

When word reached New Haven that a decade of growing tension between Great Britain and its colonies had erupted into war at Lexington and Concord in Massachusetts on April 19, 1775, New Haven's cautious town meeting voted against dispatching aid to the colonists. Benedict Arnold, captain of the Second Company of the Governor's Foot Guard, forced officials to turn over the keys to the building containing the town's store of gunpowder. He then marched his armed men to the support of the Massachusetts minutemen. It was the start of a brilliant military career that saw Arnold rise to the rank of general in the Continental Army—before turning traitor and joining the British in 1780.

During the American Revolution, New Haven was one of the targets of the devastating weeklong raid of the Connecticut coast by British, Loyalist, and Hessian troops commanded by Gen. William Tryon. The invasion took place on July 5, when a force of approximately 2,600 enemy soldiers landed on the coast early in the morning and proceeded to march up both sides of New Haven Harbor toward the heart of the community. The invaders encountered stiff resistance from local militia and civilians, including a number of Yale students, but before the day was over they reached their intended destination.

The enemy soldiers spent the next twenty-four hours plundering homes and businesses. Twenty-seven patriots were killed. The British set a few structures on fire, but most of New Haven was spared. One account claims that several local Loyalists persuaded the British not to burn the entire town. The British withdrew the next day.

The town of New Haven as originally laid out in 1638 was far larger geographically than it is today. Wallingford, which then also encompassed the modern towns of Cheshire and Meriden, became independent of New Haven in 1670. But it was after the American Revolution that new towns began peeling away from New Haven in rapid succession. Woodbridge, which then included the town of Bethany, was incorporated as a separate town in 1784. East Haven broke away in 1785, and both Hamden and North Haven in 1786. In 1822 the town of Orange, which also included modern West Haven, was formed partially out of land that had been part of New Haven.

In the decades following the Revolution New Haven enjoyed a strong maritime trade. But the arrival in 1838 of the iron horse, and the subsequent rapid expansion that made New Haven the nexus of a system of rail lines that connected with cities throughout the Northeast, spelled the beginning of the end of the city's shipping industry.

The railroad also played a key role in ushering in another major change to New Haven. Irish immigrants had been coming to the city since the early 1800s to work on digging canals. But the boom in railroad construction coincided with the devastating potato famine in Ireland in the 1840s. As a result, thousands of impoverished Irish flocked to New Haven to labor on building the new tracks. By 1850 nearly 20 percent of New Haven residents had been born in Ireland.

The Irish immigrants brought with them their Roman Catholic faith, which resulted in the founding in New Haven of what today is a global Catholic fraternal benefit society. In 1881 Father Michael McGivney met with a group of men in the basement of St. Mary's

Drawn & Engraved by J.W. Barber

E. VIEW OF THE PUBLIC SQUARE OR GREEN, IN NEW

AVEN CON.

East View of the Public Square or Green in New Haven, ca. 1831

The New Haven green had been spruced up substantially by 1831. The meetinghouse, state house, and school that had stood there in 1748 all had been razed, and almost all visible traces of the cemetery had been removed.

In the mid-1790s, the interment of many victims of a yellow fever epidemic in the green's cemetery pushed it to its capacity; at that time it included more than eight hundred gravestones and likely several times as many bodies. Burials ceased after 1812, and the cemetery became run-down.

In 1821 most of the tombstones were removed from the green and relocated to Grove Street Cemetery, established in 1797. The bodies, however, were left beneath the grass of the green, where whatever remains of them still reposes today.

Within a period of just four years, three new houses of worship had been erected adjacent to the green in a handsome row that remains one of the city's most enduring icons. They are, from left to right, Trinity Episcopal Church, Center Congregational Church, and the United Congregational Church.

Center Church, more formally the First Congregational Church, was built between 1812 and 1814. Ithiel Town, one of the early nineteenth century's most talented architects, designed it, supposedly modeling it on Sir Christopher Wren's St. Martin-in-the-Fields Church in London. Since the new meetinghouse was larger than the building it replaced, its "footprint" extended over part of the cemetery that still occupied the green. The gravestones in that section remain in place today, in the crypt beneath Center Church.

Town also designed the dramatically different Gothic Revival Trinity Episcopal Church to the left of Center Church. Completed in 1815, it was constructed of stone from New Haven's West Rock.

Connecticut architect David Hoadley designed the United Church, also completed in 1815. The explanation for how two churches of the same denomination ended up standing within a few hundred yards of each other is a case study in the contentiousness of New England Congregationalism.

Religious disagreements beginning in 1742 had created several splinter groups from the First Congregational Church. In 1796 two of these offshoots rejoined, calling themselves the United Society, which in 1815 erected a new meetinghouse right next to the home of the congregation its component members had split from decades earlier.

YALE COLLEGE & STATE HOUSE, NEW-HAVEN, CON.

Yale College and state house, New Haven, ca. 1830s

In 1829 a new state house, the third in New Haven since the city became co-capital with Hartford in 1701, was built on the green. Ithiel Town designed the Greek Revival structure, on the College Street side of the green, which meant it stood over the portion that had been used as a graveyard until 1821. Hartford became Connecticut's sole capital in 1875, and New Haven's state house was torn down in 1889.

Church to start the Knights of Columbus, which was chartered the following year by the Connecticut General Assembly. Today the organization has more than one and a half million members in more than thirteen countries. Its headquarters remain in New Haven.

By the mid-nineteenth century, the two-capital arrangement instituted in 1701 was becoming unmanageable. Connecticut government had grown and expanded along with the state and now had a plethora of offices, departments, employees, and records. Shuttling between two cities was no longer practical, and the advent of rail travel meant that no part of the state was more than a few hours by train from any other.

In 1866 the General Assembly set in motion the process of selecting a single state capital, and New Haven and Hartford engaged in a "bidding war" for the privilege. Hartford

Cingue

The Chief of the Amistad Captives

Cinque, the chief of the Amistad captives, New Haven, ca. 1840

In 1839, New Haven found itself thrust unexpectedly into the headlines of the growing movement to abolish slavery in the United States. Fifty-three Africans who had been kidnapped into slavery and shipped across the Atlantic Ocean overcame the crew of the ship Amistad, which was transporting them to a destination in Cuba. Lacking knowledge of navigation, they had to rely on one of the surviving crewmen to sail the ship, which they wanted to return to Africa. The man deceived them and managed to sail the Amistad north along the Atlantic coast in a long, meandering route until it was seized by a U.S. Navy ship off Long Island. By that time, ten of the Africans had died.

The Amistad was brought to port in New London. A short time afterward the Africans were moved to New Haven, where they spent more than a year, some confined to jail, others allowed to live with local residents, while the legal issues surrounding their case were sorted out, including whether they were guilty of murder and piracy. The Africans inspired tremendous curiosity among local residents, who paid money to see them while they were behind bars. Later the Africans were allowed to exercise on the green, where they impressed onlookers with feats of remarkable athleticism.

Northeastern abolitionists recognized the potential of the Amistad captives' story to put a human face on the case for freedom for all people, including African Americans being held in slavery. Pamphlets and newspaper articles were published about them. Portrait sketches were made of each of the Africans, as well as a striking painting of their leader, Cinque, or Cingue as this image called him. Abolitionists took the Africans to antislavery meetings around the state, where they told their story via interpreters.

New Haven lawyer Roger Sherman Baldwin represented the Amistad Africans in the Connecticut courts, and before the U.S. Supreme Court, where he was joined by former U.S. President John Quincy Adams. In 1841 the Supreme Court found the Africans innocent of the charges against them, a decision that was considered a victory for the abolitionist cause.

From New Haven the Africans went to Farmington, Connecticut, where they lived while the funds to pay their way back Africa were being raised. The thirty-five survivors finally returned to their homeland in 1842.

This lithograph of Cinque is based on a portrait painted by New Haven artist Nathaniel Jocelyn, which depicted the Amistad leader against a background dominated by West Rock.

won with an offer that included building the current State Capitol building. The General Assembly approved Hartford as the sole capital in 1873, and the voters ratified an amendment to the state constitution to that effect, to begin in 1875.

Loss of its co-capital status was a blow to New Haven's civic ego. But the city's industries flourished and multiplied, and the workers who came to the city to take jobs in the factories, including immigrants, pushed the city's population ever higher.

New Haven also still had Yale, which made great strides during the nineteenth century, adding a number of special schools, including medicine, law, divinity, music, and fine arts. Artist John Trumbull, painter of the iconic *Signing of the Declaration of Independence,*

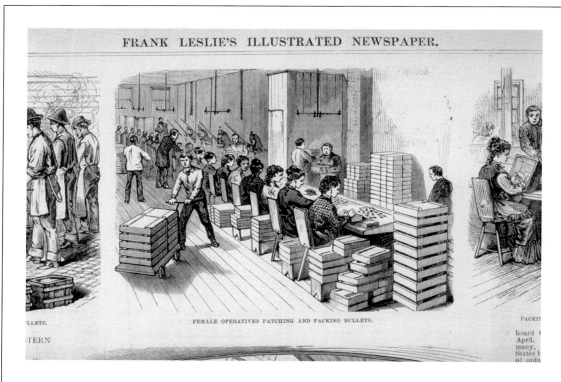

Female operatives patching and packing bullets, Winchester Metallic Cartridge Company, New Haven, 1877

New Haven manufacturing firms employed women as well as men. An 1877 illustration from Frank Leslie's Illustrated Newspaper, *a national publication, shows female workers at the Winchester Metallic Cartridge Company readying part of an order of ten million cartridges for shipment to the Turkish government.*

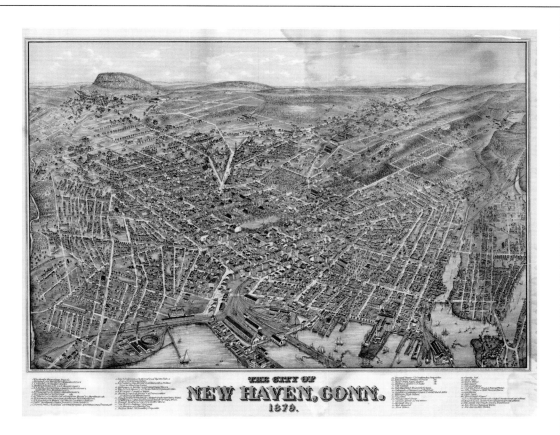

The City of New Haven, 1879

In 1879 New Haven was a city of approximately 62,000 residents, and it was dominated by massive factories that made firearms, hardware, rubber goods, locks, clocks, carriages, wire, steam engines, soap, paper boxes, and much, much more. The enormous roundhouse seen at the lower left, looking like a modern football stadium, was testimony to New Haven's importance as a hub of regional rail transportation.

in 1831 gave more than two hundred of his works to Yale to establish the Trumbull Gallery, and in 1866 George Peabody donated $150,000—equal to about $2 million in twenty-first-century dollars—to establish the Peabody Museum of Natural History.

New Haven's involvement in higher education expanded with the establishment in 1896 of the New Haven Normal School, an institution for training teachers. Today it is Southern Connecticut State University.

By 1900 New Haven had become Connecticut's most populous city, with 108,000 residents. Nearly 10 percent had been born in Ireland, 4 percent in Italy, and 3 percent in

Boys running beside horse-drawn fire wagon, Artizan Street, New Haven, ca. 1890

Few things could be guaranteed to stir more excitement among boys than firemen racing to a blaze. A trio of white horses pulls a fire wagon down Artizan Street sometime in the 1890s.

Russia. Seven hundred factories turned out everything from firearms to clocks to birdcages that were shipped via rail and water to a global market.

New Haven continued its phenomenal population and economic growth over the course of the next half century. Within two decades its population leaped from 108,000 to 162,000, largely the result of an influx of workers, including waves of immigrants from Europe, to take jobs in factories turning out materials needed to fight World War I. Also contributing to the growth of the city was the commencement of the Great Migration in which thousands of African Americans left the rural South in search of opportunities in the growing cities of the North. The city's Winchester Repeating Arms factory quadrupled its workforce, from 5,608 in 1914 to 22,000 in 1918. Its factory expanded in size to 3.25 million square feet.

Those two decades also saw the expansion of the cultural and recreational offerings in the city. The Shubert Theatre opened in 1914 and quickly became the place where

Wedding party of Giovanni Sulla and Maria Starano, New Haven, November 17, 1913

The thousands of immigrants who poured into New Haven in the early twentieth century included Giovanni Sulla and Maria Starano, both twenty-four years old, photographed on their wedding day in 1913. Giovanni, or John, as he was called in the federal census, had come to the United States around 1900, but Maria had arrived just the previous year, without her parents, who came a few years after the wedding to live with the newlyweds.

By 1930 Giovanni and Maria had done well for themselves in their new home. Giovanni, now a naturalized citizen, was a real estate broker. He and Maria and their five sons lived in a house they owned, valued at $7,000 (the equivalent of approximately $80,000 in twenty-first-century dollars), at 183 Exchange Street in New Haven.

Belt-driven machinery, C. S. Mersick and Company, ca. 1916

Employees of C. S. Mersick and Company operate machinery run by enormous wheels driven by thick belts in one of the firm's facilities around 1915. Mersick, which produced hardware and supplies for plumbers, blacksmiths, and other tradesmen, was in operation in New Haven by the late 1870s.

Broadway-bound shows would hold previews before moving on to New York. The Yale Bowl, with seating for more than 74,000, was completed that same year.

The Depression of the 1930s inflicted great hardship on New Haven residents. Many lost their jobs as manufacturers cut back. Some found work on major construction projects for Yale and for commercial and other private establishments.

New Haven factories were beginning to recover when World War II erupted. The city quickly converted to a war footing, and manufacturing surged. During the war, New Haven was a critical center for transportation of raw materials and finished goods by rail.

Despite the inevitable reduction in business following the war, in 1950 half of New Haven's workers were employed in factories. The city's population reached its all-time high that year, with 164,443 residents. Part of the increase consisted of thousands of veterans who came to New Haven to attend Yale on the G.I. Bill.

In contrast to most shoreline communities, New Haven saw its population decline precipitously during the last half of the twentieth century, dropping from that peak of 164,443 in 1950 to 126,021 by 1980. The reasons were many and varied.

Cities throughout the Northeast were hemorrhaging manufacturing jobs to parts of the country where the cost of doing business was lower, as well as to foreign countries. Industries that had formed the foundation of New Haven's economy for generations were experiencing declines in business. By 1970 just 15 percent of New Haven workers were employed in manufacturing. By 2005 it was down to less than 7 percent.

Exacerbating the exodus from New Haven was completion of the Connecticut Turnpike across the state in 1958 and of Interstate 91 in 1966. These new highways rendered the railroad largely obsolete and also made it possible for workers to live in the growing suburbs and commute by car to jobs in New Haven. The void left by thousands of departing workers was filled in part by residents of Puerto Rico who migrated to New Haven by the thousands beginning around the 1970s.

New Haven was in the forefront of urban renewal efforts in the United States beginning in the 1950s. Millions of dollars were spent on projects, with mixed results. The 1960s and 1970s, however, were decades of serious, sometimes violent, unrest in New Haven, as in many cities across the country. The 1960s were a turbulent era in American race relations, and in 1967 a riot erupted in New Haven's Hill neighborhood. Protests against the increasingly unpopular Vietnam conflict occurred on the green and at Yale. The trial in New Haven in 1970 of Bobby Seale for the murder of a fellow Black Panther generated large protests, many of them centered at Yale, and frayed relations between the city and the university. Labor strikes also were a source of tension in a city that was rapidly losing the industrial base upon which it had depended for a century.

There were other signs of flagging vitality in New Haven. The elm trees that had been its pride for nearly two centuries were largely killed off by Dutch Elm disease, assisted by the damaging winds of the hurricane of 1938. The Shubert Theatre closed in 1976.

The last decades of the twentieth century were a period of fundamental change for New Haven, as it shifted from being an industrial city to one with an economy based on providing services, in particular higher education and health care. Roughly twenty-five thousand city residents are joined every day by thirty thousand commuters, many of whom work at major institutions that include Yale, Southern Connecticut State University, Yale-New Haven Hospital, and the Hospital of Saint Raphael.

The city has witnessed a cultural revival as well. The Shubert Theatre reopened in 1983 to join the prestigious Long Wharf Theatre, established in 1965. The International Festival of Arts and Ideas, started in 1996, is an annual extravaganza of performing arts and profound thinking drawn from around the globe that also serves to highlight New Haven's rich diversity. And the elms are making a comeback. Disease-resistant specimens have been planted, interspersed with many other varieties of trees, just as centuries-old stories and traditions mingle with those of more recent vintage to create the unique character of New Haven.

12.

EAST HAVEN

$\mathcal{E}$ nglish settlement of East Haven began in 1644, and for the first three generations clustered primarily around the southern end of the long, narrow body of water that straddles the border of East Haven and Branford. Originally called simply Great Pond, it became known as Furnace Pond for the iron furnace, the first in Connecticut, that operated on its shores between 1665 and 1680. In the eighteenth century it acquired its permanent name of Lake Saltonstall, for Gurdon Saltonstall, governor of Connecticut from 1708 to 1724, who had purchased a farm on the lake's shore.

East Haven was set off as a separate religious parish within New Haven in 1709, and in 1785 it was incorporated as an independent town. But the contours of the town were strikingly different from what they are today; as originally set out, East Haven's western boundary was New Haven Harbor and the Quinnipiac River.

The new town's population increased slowly but steadily for the next half century. Then between 1840 and 1860 it abruptly experienced a dramatic spike from 1,382 to 2,292. More than 150 refugees from the Irish potato famine, and the children they bore in America, accounted for much of this 65 percent increase.

East Haven's contributions toward the cost of the Civil War left the town owing enormous amounts of money. Paying for all or part of the cost of five bridges sank it even deeper into debt. By 1881, the town of three thousand owed more than $200,000—the equivalent of more than $4 million in twenty-first-century money.

To get out from under that crushing financial burden, East Haven cut an unusual deal with its neighbor New Haven in 1881. New Haven would assume all of East Haven's Civil War and bridge construction debts; in return, East Haven agreed to cede the western half of the town to New Haven.

The arrangement was put to the people, and the citizens of East Haven voted by a margin of more than four to one in favor of the drastic measure of cutting the town's

N. Western view of the Congregational and Episcopal churches East Haven

Northwestern view of the Congregational and Episcopal churches, East Haven ca. 1835

When it came time to erect a new meetinghouse in 1774, East Haven Congregationalists made an unusual decision for the simplest of reasons. They built the structure of stone, an almost unheard-of material for that time in Connecticut, because it could be quarried locally and thus cost less than the traditional wood.

Great progress had been made, but the house of worship was not finished when the American Revolution broke out in 1775. The war not only delayed completion of the building indefinitely, it marched right up to—and through—the meetinghouse's door. When the British invaded New Haven in July of 1779, enemy soldiers plundered the East Haven meetinghouse of its silver communion service before local militia drove them off.

Placement of a tall spire atop the meetinghouse signaled its long-overdue completion in 1796. The very next year a tornado ripped the steeple off the building. It didn't fall to the ground, but crashed through the roof, causing extensive damage. Undaunted, the congregation quickly replaced it with a better, stronger specimen, the one seen in this drawing of the center of East Haven in 1835.

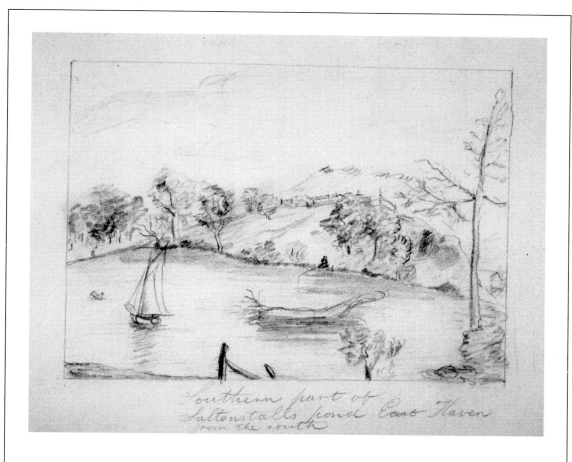

Southern part of Saltonstalls pond, East Haven from the south, ca. 1835

A small sailboat skims along the surface of Lake Saltonstall's southern end in an 1835 sketch. Later in the nineteenth century an amusement park was built on the lake, but it was closed in 1896, when the lake was designated a source of public water for New Haven and other area towns. More than a century later Lake Saltonstall continues to serve that purpose, as part of the South Central Connecticut Regional Water Authority's more than 26,000 acres of watershed and aquifer lands.

size by half as a solution to its fiscal woes. The transfer was completed the following year.

Two-thirds of East Haven's population lived in the area annexed by New Haven. That left the geographically leaner East Haven with fewer than one thousand residents.

It was not long, however, before the town experienced another growth spurt even bigger than the one during the two decades prior to the Civil War. Population nearly

Foxon Road, July 20, 1895

Foxon Road, today a major transportation artery, was just a stretch of dry, hard-packed dirt when this photograph was taken in 1895. Although the scene is late July, the man perched on the rail fence still wears his coat and bowler hat.

Connecticut Company outing, Momauguin, sack race, August 1916

Connecticut Company outing, Momauguin, broad jump, August 1916

Employees of the Connecticut Company competed at the broad jump and in a sack race during an outing in August 1916 at Momauguin, which probably refers to the beach of that name along Long Island Sound in East Haven. The Connecticut Company operated a large portion of the trolley lines that ran along the state's coastline during the first half of the twentieth century.

Congregational church, 1940s

The stone Congregational meetinghouse that withstood British marauders and nature's fury also held its own against the onslaught of the twentieth-century automobile culture, with its paved roads, heavy vehicles, and gasoline pumps, as this 1940s photograph testifies. "The Old Stone Church," as it has come to be called, still stands in East Haven. It is the oldest surviving stone church in Connecticut and one of the oldest houses of worship of any material in the state.

doubled between 1890 and 1910, then nearly doubled again between 1910 and 1920, and again between 1920 and 1930.

This phenomenal growth was largely attributable to the same cause as the earlier one: the arrival of immigrants who put down roots and started families. Italian immigrants began arriving late in the 1800s, and their numbers increased dramatically over the next several decades. The combination of Irish and Italians resulted in enough Roman Catholics in East Haven to justify the establishment of a parish, St. Vincent de Paul, in 1914.

By 1930 East Haven had large numbers of first- and second-generation Italians and Poles. The town was also home to smaller numbers of residents who had been born in more than half a dozen other countries, including Sweden, Germany, Russia, Lithuania, Denmark, and Hungary.

Following World War II, East Haven felt the impact of both the baby boom and the movement of families out of cities into smaller communities. The construction of the Connecticut Turnpike (Interstate 95) made it a short commute from East Haven to New Haven. As a result, East Haven's population once again grew by leaps and bounds, more than doubling between 1950 and 1970 before leveling off at 25,000 in the 1970s. The decades since have seen only small increases in the number of East Haven residents. East Haven has one of the highest proportions of residents of Italian descent—50 percent—of any town in the United States.

13.

BRANFORD

*I*t took English colonists two tries to settle Branford in the 1600s. Why two tries? Stubborn unwillingness to compromise.

The first English arrived in Branford in 1644. They were a splinter group of residents of Wethersfield, Connecticut, whose people had been split over religious issues from its very founding more than a decade earlier. It having become clear that the breach would never be healed, one faction decided to move to Branford to start fresh. They were joined by some Congregationalists from Long Island, then part of the Connecticut Colony, led by the Reverend Abraham Pierson, who became the first pastor of the Branford Congregational church.

The next two decades passed without major incident. Then in 1665 the New Haven Colony, to which Branford belonged, was absorbed by the Connecticut Colony to the north, under the terms of the charter granted to the Connecticut Colony by King Charles II.

Branford residents were unhappy about the involuntary merger, perhaps because the Connecticut Colony was not as strict a Puritan theocracy as the New Haven Colony had been. "Mr. Pierson and almost his whole church and congregation were so displeased, that they soon removed to Newark, in New Jersey," in 1667, wrote Connecticut historian John Warner Barber. Their departure left Branford "almost without inhabitants."

Newcomers trickled into Branford "so that in about twenty years it became resettled," noted Barber. In 1685 Branford "was reinvested with town privileges," and in 1687 the Congregational church was reorganized.

Over the next 150 years, Branford developed into primarily an agricultural community. Some trade took place with ports along the Atlantic coast and the West Indies, and a significant shipbuilding industry operated from the turn of the nineteenth century until the Civil War.

West view of the Congregational and Episcopal churches and Academy in Branford, ca. 1835

Of the three structures standing on the Branford green in 1835, only the building in the middle background, built in 1830 as the private Branford Academy, still stands—although some distance from its original site. The Congregational meetinghouse with the soaring spire and clock had been built in 1741. It was torn down in 1843 to make way for the church that is there today. The modest building to the left was Trinity Episcopal Church. Although it had been established as a mission of the Church of England in 1748, a house of worship wasn't built until 1784. This building was replaced in 1851 by the current building.

In 1750, the Congregationalists allowed the Episcopalians, or Anglicans, as they were then called, to celebrate Christmas in the meetinghouse. This was no small indulgence, considering that Congregationalists themselves made a point of not observing Christmas in any way.

The arrival of the railroad in 1852 was quickly followed by development of a significant manufacturing base in Branford. In 1854 the Totoket Company was founded to produce "malleable iron"—very strong iron that can be fashioned into items by beating

Sam's first store in Branford, ca. 1890

Sam Griswold's store in Branford, shown around the turn of the twentieth century, was a full-service establishment. Sam sold baby carriages for infants just starting out on life and also provided undertaking services for those who had reached the end of their earthly sojourn.

or rolling. The Totoket Company was sold in 1864 to new owners who renamed the firm Malleable Iron Fittings.

For a century Malleable Iron Fittings—or MIF in local shorthand—turned out a wide line of products, from oil burners to sewing machines to mortar shells. But the company encountered rough times in the 1950s and 1960s, caused by a combination of decreased demand for its products and competition from foreign firms that could pay their workers much less. In 1971, MIF shut down for good. Other important industries in the town's history have included the Branford Lock Works, the Atlantic Wire Company, and the Nutmeg Crucible Steel Company.

Granite quarries began opening in Branford around the time of the Civil War. Over the next sixty years stone from Branford was used to construct municipal and commercial

Workmen in quarry with stone for Bulkeley Bridge, ca. 1904

Four laborers and two businessmen (judging from their clothes) confer atop a block of granite destined to become part of the Bulkeley Bridge in Hartford, today part of Interstate 84. The bridge across the Connecticut River, completed in 1908, was constructed of stone from quarries at two sites in Branford, Leete's Island and Stony Creek, with the photograph probably depicting the latter.

Thimble Islands, ca. 1910

Following the Civil War, Branford's Thimble Islands became popular locations for resort hotels and summer cottages. There are one hundred or so Thimble Islands—depending upon what definition of island one chooses to use. Today there are approximately eighty houses on fewer than two dozen islands.

    The largest occupied island is Money Island, with a community of thirty-two houses and a library. More than a dozen islands offer the solitude—or isolation—of only a single house on them. That level of privacy has made the Thimble Islands attractive to celebrities for well over a century.

    The Thimble Islands' desirable location proved deadly in September of 1938, when the worst hurricane in New England history struck without warning. Seven Thimble Island occupants died in the storm, including five who were swept away when a monstrous tidal surge completely destroyed a house on Jepson Island.

Bird's-eye view of Branford, 1905

The opening of several large manufacturing operations, the development of a number of large quarries, and the flourishing of establishments that catered to a large influx of summer vacationers during the last half of the nineteenth century turned Branford from a village into a bustling town. The population had quadrupled since 1850, to approximately six thousand. Another small but telling change: Automobiles had begun to make their appearance on Branford streets.

The town's great pride is depicted at the top center of the view: the grand new James Blackstone Memorial Library. The building, completed in 1896, was made of Tennessee marble at a reported cost of $300,000—more than $7 million in twenty-first-century dollars.

Malleable Iron Fittings——or MIF, as it was more conveniently referred to——seen in the vignette at the bottom of the view, established in 1854, had by this time expanded to become one of Branford's major employers. In subsequent decades, when Branford's population ranged between 7,000 and 8,000, as many as 1,200 people had jobs at MIF. Many were immigrants, some of whom had ended up in Branford because MIF representatives went to the waterfront in New York City to recruit workers from among the new arrivals right off the boat.

Ella Wheeler Wilcox.

Ella Wheeler Wilcox, 1892

Ella Wheeler Wilcox was famous at the turn of the twentieth century as the "poetess of passion," and there were few things about which she was more passionate than her home at Short Beach on Granite Bay. Beginning in 1891, Wilcox spent summers at the house she built and called "The Bungalow." With construction in 1906 of a second building fitted out for winter, called "The Barracks," Short Beach became Wilcox's permanent, year-round residence for the rest of her life.

Born in Wisconsin in 1850, Wilcox achieved international fame with the publication in 1883 of her work Poems of Passion. *A Chicago publisher to whom she sent the manuscript sent it back, "intimating it was immoral," recalled Wilcox. The story was quickly reported in newspapers across the country. When another Chicago publisher issued the book, the notoriety of that first publisher's comment helped it sell sixty thousand copies in two years.*

Wilcox ultimately wrote more than seventy books, including poetry, fiction, and nonfiction. In addition to being a prolific author, she immersed herself in popular movements and philosophies of the era that included, sometimes in combination, mysticism, spiritualism, psychic research, meditation, and positive thinking.

Wilcox enjoyed parties and entertaining. She and her husband welcomed to their Short Beach home celebrities including actor John Barrymore, author Jack London, and botanist Luther Burbank. Wilcox established the annual tradition of an August "Illumination Night," when Short Beach homes, docks, and boats were festooned with colored lanterns.

The year before she died, Wilcox put her affection for the Short Beach home she considered her "earthly Eden" into verse in the poem titled "Granite Bay":

> *Though forth my wandering footsteps stray,*
> *To realms and regions far away,*
> *My heart dwells here, in Granite Bay.*

Many of Ella Wheeler Wilcox's books remain in print today, including Poems of Passion, *the one that started it all. In recent years, Short Beach residents have once again begun celebrating "Illumination Night." The Labor Day weekend event is complete with decorative lanterns, music, dancing, and readings of Wilcox's poetry.*

SHORE AND THE BUNGALOW, SHORT BEACH, BRANFORD, CONN.

Shore and the Bungalow, Short Beach (Ella Wheeler Wilcox House), ca. 1901–1907

buildings from New York City to New Orleans to Chicago, including Grand Central Station. Monuments made of Branford granite included Grant's Tomb in New York and the massive column erected in 1893 at West Point to commemorate the academy's graduates who lost their lives in the Civil War.

Immigrants made up much of the labor force in both the factories and the quarries. The newcomers from Italy, Ireland, Sweden, Finland, England, Scotland, Spain, and Eastern European countries introduced a strong multicultural component to life in Branford.

In the mid-1800s Branford began to emerge as a popular summer resort, conveniently accessible to New Haven, New York, and other cities by train, trolley, or boat. The town's twenty waterfront hotels could accommodate hundreds of vacationers at a time. Many more rented or built their own cottages. Several of these establishments and summer houses were situated on various of the Thimble Islands, where at times yachts by the dozens would be anchored.

Farm River Motor Boat Club, Short Beach, Conn.

Farm River Motor Boat Club (later Nellie Green House), ca. 1910

Nellie Green Talmadge smuggled her way into Short Beach legend. For more than a decade, she over-saw an operation that imported illegal alcoholic beverages into Connecticut.

Nellie's father and grandfather began running an inn, built in 1901, on Short Beach Road on the Branford side of the Farm River, which serves as the border with East Haven. By 1910 Nellie and her husband, William Talmadge, were living on Short Beach Road in East Haven. For the next twenty years at least, the couple lived in East Haven, while William worked as an ice or coal dealer and Nellie ran the inn across the Farm River that her father and grandfather had operated. For a time it was known as the Talmadge Hotel, but eventually it came to be called "Nellie Green's."

In 1920 the Eighteenth Amendment to the U.S. Constitution prohibited the manufacture, sale, or transport of alcoholic beverages, ushering in the era that would be known as Prohibition. Nellie Green Talmadge saw in the ban a business opportunity and proceeded to open a speakeasy in her Branford hotel. She branched out, reportedly overseeing a flotilla of nine boats that smuggled illegal liquor up the Farm River from Long Island Sound to her hotel, where it was stashed. Nellie Green Talmadge's reputation as a successful rumrunner spread up and down the East Coast. Curiously—or perhaps tellingly—William and Nellie's son Charles, who was living with his parents in 1930, was listed in the census as being employed in the beverage industry, specifically "ginger ale."

Prohibition ended in 1933, and Nellie continued to run her hotel as a popular watering hole that included among its patrons such celebrities as actors John Barrymore, Rudy Vallee, Tyrone Power, and Bing Crosby. Nellie died in 1952, but the building that was the center of her colorful operations—legal and illegal—still stands near the bridge where generations of teenagers have jumped into the Farm River.

The waters around the Thimble Islands provided another boon to Branford in the decades at the turn of the twentieth century: an abundance of prime oysters that were specialties of several of the resorts.

The summer visitors, the quarries, and the oysters all began to decline after World War I. Only one quarry remains open in Branford today. All but a couple of the grand resorts had been closed, converted into residences, or torn or burned down by the 1970s. Manufacturing lost its prominence in the last decades of the twentieth century, to be replaced to a degree by high-tech firms.

During the last half of the twentieth century, Branford, like many other shoreline communities, acquired a new role as a convenient place for people who worked in cities like New Haven to have their homes. The town's population nearly tripled, from 10,944 in 1950 to 28,683 in 2000.

14.

GUILFORD

*W*ith more than 450 historic buildings and thousands of acres of pastures, meadows, fields, and forests, Guilford evokes the romantic vision and traditional values of classic New England as few towns can. The town green, surrounded by dozens of structures of varying sizes and ages, is reminiscent of a table around which generations of a family have come together. The stately white First Congregational meetinghouse at the head of the green, its steeple rising above all other buildings, is the venerable paterfamilias presiding over the gathering.

One of Connecticut's oldest towns, Guilford was established in 1639 by a band of 350 English Puritans under the leadership of the Reverend Henry Whitfield. Its original boundaries included what is today the town of Madison.

The Guilford coast's lack of a harbor deep enough to accommodate large sailing vessels prevented it from developing into a major colonial shipping port like New Haven or New London. From the original seed of settlement near the coast, subsequent generations pushed inland. Within a century parts of town farthest from the Sound had been settled.

Dozens of Guilford men marched off to serve in the war for independence from Great Britain that erupted at Lexington and Concord in 1775. More than two dozen died. On two occasions the fighting came literally to Guilford's doorsteps.

In the summer of 1776, the enemy British gained control of Long Island—so close to Guilford that its shore is visible on a clear day. Redcoat raiders came ashore at Sachem's Head on June 17, 1777, but succeeded only in burning down a house and barns before the townspeople forced them to retreat. On June 18, 1781, three British vessels deposited a force of 150 men on Leete's Island. Residents repelled the invaders in a skirmish that left two Guilford men dead.

Southwest view of the ancient Stone House in Guilford, ca. 1835

Women on the home front contributed to the war effort as well. Lyman Beecher, father of Harriet Beecher Stowe, was a boy in North Guilford during the Revolution. He recalled how the women of the household spun flax and wool into yarn from which "they made all sorts of linen work, table-cloths, shirting, sheets, and cloths. If it hadn't been for this household manufactory we never should have succeeded in the Revolution."

During the half century following the American Revolution, small Connecticut towns saw a massive exodus of people seeking fresh land and opportunity on far-flung frontiers, including Vermont, New York, and Ohio. Guilford avoided the drastic decline in population experienced by so many communities, although it was reduced in size by nearly half when the eastern portion broke off to become the town of Madison in 1826.

Guilford did feel the impact of other changes in the years preceding the Civil War. The controversial crusade to abolish slavery throughout the United States roiled and finally rent the membership of the First Congregational Church. In 1843, 123 members who supported abolition broke away to form a new congregation, and they built their own house of worship, the Third Congregational Church, a short distance away on Park Street.

Henry Whitfield House, ca. 1920–1940

The Henry Whitfield State Museum is a sentinel from Guilford's origin as a frontier settlement and a testament to the extraordinary passion for the past that has made the entire town a case study of successful historic preservation. Built in 1639, it is the oldest house in Connecticut and the oldest stone house in New England.

The building was meant to serve two purposes. It was home to the Reverend Henry Whitfield, leader of the Puritans who settled Guilford. And with its three-foot-thick granite walls and clear view of Long Island Sound from the second floor, it was also intended to serve as a fortress to which residents could retreat in the event of attack by enemies, who included the Dutch from nearby New Amsterdam or Native Americans from outside the region.

The State of Connecticut purchased the "Ancient Stone House" in 1899 and soon afterward opened it as the first state museum. In the 1930s pioneering architectural historian J. Frederick Kelly conducted a thorough investigation of the building, which had been significantly altered by its occupants over the course of three centuries.

Kelly's research revealed that only the exterior stone walls were original to 1639. He removed the stucco that had been applied to them decades before the earliest known image of the house was rendered in 1835.

Not enough evidence had survived to make it possible to faithfully reproduce the Stone House's interior to its appearance in 1639. That was not an insurmountable obstacle, however, for Kelly was working during the Colonial Revival, when historic buildings were restored as much to evoke the admirable values and qualities of earlier generations as to accurately re-create what originally existed. Kelly replaced all the interior finishings with materials appropriate to 1639, based on his research, comparison to similar buildings in England, and educated guesses.

In 1997 the Henry Whitfield State Museum was declared a National Historic Landmark, as "an example of Colonial Revival restoration work that stands as a testament to the historic preservation movement in America."

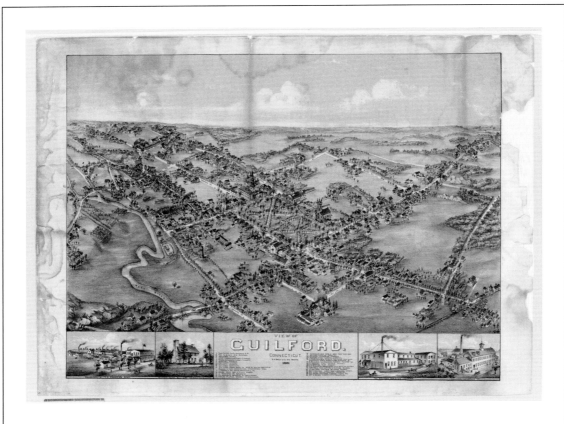

View of Guilford, 1881

Dozens of buildings depicted on this 1881 bird's-eye view of Guilford still stand, their appearance little changed by the passage of 125 years. The vignettes at the bottom highlight three of nineteenth-century Guilford's largest manufacturers: the Guilford Enterprise Company, the Guilford Canning Company, and I. S. Spencer's Sons.

Sixty-two sons of Guilford, some still in their teens, died in the Civil War, precipitated in large part by the controversy over slavery that had split the First Congregational Church. They fell on the legendary battlefields of Gettysburg, Antietam, Petersburg, and Chancellorsville, among others.

Guilford lacked the rapid streams that energetic entrepreneurs in other parts of the state used to power new mills and factories during the nineteenth century, but the arrival of the railroad in 1852 did provide a small shot in the arm for local manufacturing. With an efficient method of shipping now available, several factories sprang up, including the Knowles Lombard Company, which packed hundreds of thousands of cans of tomatoes each year. The most enduring factory was the I. S. Spencer Company foundry, but Guilford never became home to a major factory or industry that attracted floods of immigrants and transformed such cities as Bridgeport, Waterbury, and Hartford into urban behemoths.

The quarry that spans the Guilford/Branford boundary became an important economic resource, attracting immigrant workers from Italy and Scandinavia to join the small number of Irish already settled in town. The Leete's Island Quarry supplied the pink granite used to construct the eighty-nine-foot-tall pedestal of the Statue of Liberty between 1884 and 1886.

Train travel also made Guilford a convenient destination for city dwellers seeking the tranquil beauty of the shore and the countryside for vacations. Several shoreline resorts

Workers in front of I. S. Spencer's Sons Iron Founders & Manufacturers building, 1880

One of the few large-scale industries to operate successfully in Guilford during the nineteenth and twentieth centuries was I. S. Spencer's Sons. An iron foundry, the firm opened in 1857 and closed in 1981. Part of the brick manufacturing facility, in front of which several dozen employees posed for this 1880 photo, still stands on Fair Street. Immigrants, including the Irish who began arriving in Guilford in the mid-1800s, as well as a few members of the town's small African-American population, found work here making products that included legs for school desks, lamp pedestals, and bicycle parts.

Guilford green, 1881

In 1881, the Guilford green was essentially the same beautiful public space people enjoy and admire today. Modern landmarks visible in this detail taken from the bird's-eye view published that year include the 1830 Greek Revival First Congregational Church, its soaring spire dominating the green, and the 1838 Gothic Revival Christ Episcopal Church, with its handsome square stone tower.

But for the first two centuries after the green was laid out in 1639, it was not a parklike green space but a public meeting site where just about every imaginable community activity took place. In 1800, Yale President Timothy Dwight wrote of the Guilford green that "two churches, a Presbyterian and an Episcopal, stand on it, together with four schoolhouses." In addition to those six buildings, Dwight noted disapprovingly, the green was "deformed by a burying ground, and to add to the deformity is unenclosed. The graves are therefore trampled upon and the monuments injured by both men and cattle."

What Dwight witnessed was only part of the activity that had occurred on the Guilford green. At various times in its history it had also been the site of a hay scale, saw and gravel pits, and a whipping post. Not just cows, but horses, pigs, and sheep were turned loose by their owners, with the town's permission, to graze among the structures and the gravestones.

Efforts to clean up the cluttered, gritty green began in the second decade of the nineteenth century. In 1824 the gravestones were removed and placed in newer cemeteries—but the bodies apparently were left to moulder in place. Livestock were no longer permitted to run at large. A wooden fence was erected around the green in 1837, and the last of the buildings was removed by 1838. The now-clear space was planted with one hundred elm trees.

The campaign to spruce up the green gained momentum with the establishment in 1874 of the United Workers for Public Improvement, a women's organization that for the next fifty-seven years was dedicated to beautifying the town in general and the green in particular. Their inaugural spring cleanup each year was marked by cannon fire, ringing of church bells, and band music.

The construction in 1877 of a statue honoring Guilford men who died in the Civil War established the green as the place where monuments to those who gave their lives in subsequent conflicts would be erected. The wooden fence came down in 1899. Most of the elms seen in the 1881 bird's-eye-view fell in the hurricane of 1938 but have been replaced with now-mature maple trees.

were established to cater to tourists, including the Sachem's Head Hotel. Lodges sprang up around Lake Quonnipaug in the northern end of town.

Guilford experienced relatively little change in the half century between 1880 and 1930. Its population was essentially static, hovering around 2,800. A stagnant population and economy provide little incentive or money for replacing old buildings with new homes, factories, or businesses. That reality, along with the rerouting of the Boston Post Road—today's Route 1, which subsequently became the focus of most commercial development—away from the town green in the 1920s, had the happy effect of saving many historic structures from the wrecking ball.

The baby boom, a thriving post-war economy, construction of the Connecticut Turnpike (Interstate 95) in 1957, and the movement of families out of cities into new suburban developments following World War II were major transforming events for Guilford.

The Rustic Inn, Lake Quonnipaug, ca. 1900–1930

The shoreline wasn't the only part of Guilford that found favor with vacationers. Resorts like the Rustic Inn on the shores of Lake Quonnipaug in the northern end of town attracted hunters, anglers, canoeists, and seekers of the serenity of nature.

Grass Island, Guilford, 2008. Photo by Diana Ross McCain

The solitary fishing shack that has stood on Guilford Harbor's Grass Island for decades is one of the more recent—and much-photographed—additions to the town's picturesque landscape.

Fitz-Greene Halleck, one of nineteenth-century America's most popular poets, whose romantic writing earned him the nickname the "American Byron," was born in a house on the Guilford green in 1790 and spent the last twenty years of his life in the house at 25 Water Street. Halleck could very well have had Guilford in mind when he penned his poem "Connecticut." Published in 1826, it includes these lines:

Her clear, warm heaven at noon,——the mist that shrouds
Her twilight hills——her cool and starry eves,
The glorious splendor of her sunset clouds,
The rainbow beauty of her forest leaves,
Com o'er the eye, in solitude and crowds,
Where're his web of song her poet weaves;
And his mind's brightest vision but displays
The autumn scenery of his boyhood's days.

The town's population skyrocketed, quadrupling from 5,092 in 1950 to 21,298 in 2000, as people who worked in New Haven and other communities moved to Guilford.

Many different groups have worked hard—and continue to work—to maintain a balance between the recent juggernaut of residential and commercial growth and preservation of the historic buildings and rural landscape that embody Guilford's centuries-old heritage. Guilford has four historic districts listed on the National Register of Historic Places and boasts one of the largest number of eighteenth-century houses in the nation.

15.

MADISON

Every year a million visitors flock to Madison's Hammonasset Beach, the state's largest shoreline park, to play in the sand and salt water. Hammonasset has been a high-profile feature of Madison for more than eighty years, but there's much more to the town's history than fun in the sun—including a fabulously rich philanthropist and a fallen defender of freedom.

Madison was part of Guilford when the first English settlers arrived in the area along the shoreline around 1650. The northern portion of town "remained a wilderness," in the words of one historian, until about 1725. In 1703 what would become Madison was set aside as the East Guilford religious society.

As is true of nearly every town on the Connecticut coast, life during Madison's first two hundred years was centered around farming, shipbuilding, seafaring, and fishing. But dramatic incidents occasionally punctuated the daily routine.

During the American Revolution, British ships harassed Madison, and one impromptu defense against an enemy incursion turned deadly. When the United States found itself once more at war with Great Britain more than forty years later, a Madison man earned a reputation as a daring defender of the coast.

During the War of 1812, Capt. Frederick Lee commanded the *Eagle,* a revenue cutter (as vessels in the branch of service that was a forerunner of the U.S. Coast Guard were called). The *Eagle* sailed Long Island Sound, on the lookout for enemy vessels or Americans trading illegally with the British. Captain Lee captured three of the latter—and then his luck ran out.

On the Sound on October 11, 1814, the *Eagle* challenged two British ships attempting to seize an American vessel and drove them away from their intended prey. Captain Lee was then forced to retreat before the superior firepower of the British ships. The *Eagle* was

Capt. Phineas Meigs's hat, 1782

British ships prowling Long Island Sound during the waning days of the American Revolution forced a small patriot-owned vessel aground at Madison on May 19, 1782. Enemy redcoats boarded the stranded ship, bent on capturing it.

A band of local men, equipped with one small cannon, confronted the marauders, killing one and wounding several before they at last retreated without their prize. Madison's defenders suffered one fatality: militia captain Phineas Meigs, a seventy-three-year-old grandfather, who was killed by a musket ball to the head that left gaping holes in his hat.

driven aground on the north shore of Long Island, at a spot roughly across the Sound from Branford, Connecticut. Refusing to admit defeat, the men of the *Eagle* dragged the ship's cannon to the top of Friar's Head, a 160-foot-high bluff, and resumed the battle. The British retreated, and Captain Lee regained possession of his damaged ship. But before he could find safe harbor, the British returned and seized the *Eagle*.

It was local war hero Captain Lee who reportedly named the new town that was carved out of the eastern portion of Guilford in 1826. It was called Madison in honor of James Madison, president of the United States from 1809 to 1817.

During the nineteenth century Madison sent forth into the world visionaries who made history while remaining connected to their roots. One of these was Cornelius Bushnell, born in 1829 in the Allis-Bushnell House, today home to the Madison Historical Society. At age sixteen Cornelius Bushnell was captain of a coastal schooner. After five years at sea he settled in New Haven, where he and his brother built up the largest maritime hardware firm in the state.

Lee's Academy and Congregational Church in Madison, ca. 1835

Lee's Academy and Congregational Church in Madison, ca. 1835

The building in the center of this 1835 sketch of the Madison town green is the Lee Academy, established in 1821. It was named for Madison's war hero, Capt. Frederick Lee, who contributed half of the $1,200 construction cost. The school attracted students from as far away as New York City and New Orleans.

At the time of its construction, it was stipulated that the Lee Academy would never be moved, but that requirement had already been violated by the time this sketch was drawn. It had been moved in 1831 from its original site at the corner of Boston Post Road and Neck Road, across from Captain Lee's home, to the location shown in the sketch. Four years later it moved again, to the opposite side of the green. The academy's classes were conducted on the upper floor, with public school classes held on the first floor.

Over the next decades, the academy gradually came under town control. In 1877 Madison joined the trend toward public secondary education by funding a high school for local students twelve years and up to be held in Lee's Academy.

With the opening of the Daniel Hand Academy in 1884, the Lee Academy ceased operation. The building was moved yet again in 1896 to a spot near the Hand Academy. It continued to serve as a public school until 1922.

In 1923 the building that wasn't ever supposed to be moved was relocated a fourth time, to its current site, at the eastern edge of Meetinghouse Lane, facing west toward the green. It was taken over by the Madison Historical Society, which today presents exhibitions and programs there.

Copyright 1905 by the Rotograph Co.
A 5405 Hand Academy, Madison, Conn.

Daniel Hand Academy, ca. 1884–1921

In 1884 wealthy businessman Daniel Hand spent $15,000—the equivalent of more than $300,000 in twenty-first-century dollars—to construct this building for his native Madison to use as an academy. In 1897 the town made the Hand Academy a free school, and in 1921 it became the Hand Consolidated School, the forerunner of Madison's modern Daniel Hand High School, built in 1960.

Generous as Hand's gift was, he was just getting warmed up as a philanthropist.

Born in 1801, Daniel Hand moved in his teens to Georgia, where he lived for the next thirty-five years, building a thriving interstate grocery business. In 1854 he relocated to New York City to serve as purchasing agent for his firm, leaving the Southern operations in his partner's hands.

When the Civil War erupted in April of 1861, Hand returned South to help protect his business interests, which were in danger of being confiscated by the Confederates due to Hand's open opposition to secession. Despite having lived in Georgia for decades, Hand, newly arrived from New York, was considered a "Yankee." He was twice jailed on suspicion of being a spy, and once he had to be rescued from an angry mob.

Hand spent the rest of the war quietly in North Carolina. When the conflict ended, he returned North to live with relatives in Guilford, determined to never again set foot on Southern soil.

In 1881 Hand, now eighty, was worth between $30 and $40 million in twenty-first-century dollars. His wife and all his children were dead, so he set about disposing of his wealth. After demonstrating that "charity begins at home" with his gift of the academy to Madison, Hand in 1888 gave the equivalent of $20 million in modern money to the American Missionary Society for a fund to educate African Americans living in states in which slavery existed in 1861. It was the largest donation made up to that time by a living benefactor to an American charity. When Hand died in 1891 he left additional funds, the equivalent of approximately $10 million in today's money, to be added to his original donation to the American Missionary Society.

Daniel Hand understood that Southern blacks, especially emancipated slaves, required education in order to be self-sufficient. His gifts have generated total income in excess of $6 million that has helped support more than 125 primary schools for African Americans, as well as six historically black colleges, in a dozen Southern states.

Boston Post Road, West from Library, Madison, Conn.

Boston Post Road from front of Scranton library, ca. 1920–1930

By the 1920s the automobile was gaining ground as the preferred form of transportation, but cars had not yet rendered horse-drawn buggies and oxcarts obsolete, as this photograph of the Boston Post Road from a vantage point in front of the E. C. Scranton Library shows.

By the mid-1930s, Madison had become "the discovery of the decade, among the leisurely wealthy," according to a New Haven Register *reporter. That popularity as a getaway inevitably brought with it a heavy increase in traffic, a more commercial character to the town, and a more hectic pace of life.*

In 1858 Bushnell invested in the New Haven and New London Railroad, of which he soon became president. In that job he lobbied officials on the state and federal levels, which led to his most remarkable achievement.

Soon after the Civil War erupted in April of 1861, the federal government learned the Confederates were developing a new kind of battleship, one clad in iron that would repel cannonballs and pose a terrible danger to the Union Navy's wooden-hulled vessels. Secretary of the Navy Gideon Welles, a former Connecticut newspaper editor, knew of Bushnell from his politicking for the railroad before the General Assembly and Congress. At Welles's request, Bushnell handled the delicate job of getting Congress to approve $1.5

million for the Union's own ironclad, the *Monitor,* then supervised its construction. The *Monitor* was launched on January 30, 1862, with a crew of 320, and went immediately in search of a confrontation with the Confederate ironclad, the *Merrimac.*

The *Merrimac* had spent the day of March 8 savaging wooden-hulled Union vessels in the Virginia harbor of Hampton Roads like a wolf rampaging among sheep. The *Monitor* arrived after dark, and the next day the two ironclads clashed in an epic battle that, although it ended in a draw, marked the beginning of an entirely new chapter of naval warfare.

After the war, Cornelius Bushnell refocused on railroading. He became a major investor in the Union Pacific Railroad, which at the famous 1869 "golden spike" ceremony

Short-term camps, Hammonasset Beach State Park, ca. 1930s

Hammonasset Beach opened as a six-hundred-acre state park in 1920. It attracted day-trippers as well as campers from as far away as California, Texas, and Florida, like those set up in this photograph, probably taken in the decade prior to World War II.

During World War II, the park was closed and converted to an army reservation. Military airplanes from Bradley Field in Windsor Locks practiced shooting at targets on Meigs Point—firing in the direction of Long Island Sound, for safety's sake.

Hammonasset reopened following the war and continued to expand. Today it contains more than a thousand acres, including two miles of beach.

was connected to the Central Pacific Railroad, creating the first transcontinental rail line.

By the end of the nineteenth century, Madison was well on the way to becoming a popular vacation spot. "The magnificent stretch of hard sand beach, the glory of the town, extending for some five miles, early proved attractive to summer visitors," historian Bernard Steiner wrote in 1897. The first vacation cottage was built in 1867; forty years later there were three hundred. Businesses that sprang up to supply the needs of seasonal visitors became an important sector of the local economy.

The post–War World II baby boom, the spread of suburbanization, and, especially in Madison's case, completion of the Connecticut Turnpike (modern Interstate 95) in the 1950s resulted in a massive growth spurt for the town. From its incorporation in 1826 until 1930, Madison's population had fluctuated between 1,500 and 1,800 residents, never exceeding 2,000. But beginning in 1940, the population grew by leaps and bounds. It doubled between 1940 and 1960, doubled again between 1960 and 1970, and grew another 50 percent between 1970 and 1980. Since then it has experienced much slower, but still steady, growth.

A MOTLEY GROUP
OF LIGHTHOUSES

For two centuries lighthouses along Connecticut's rocky coast have helped mariners navigate Long Island Sound's treacherous reefs, shoals, ledges, and other natural and man-made threats, in fair weather and foul, in darkness and daylight. The always-reliable guidance they have provided to those contending year in and year out with the dangerous unpredictability of nature and fate has made lighthouses cherished symbols of strength and stability in a world of rapid, constant, sometimes chaotic change.

Like an early-morning fog, an aura of mystery and romance has hovered over the men and more than a few women who have tended lighthouses. They lived in an isolation that for some was welcome solitude, for others sterile loneliness that drove them literally insane. They possessed the courage and stamina to live on the front lines of the never-ending battle with the elements. Ever vigilant, they kept signal fires burning bright. And on the countless occasions when, despite all precautions, vessels still foundered, they risked their own lives to save literally hundreds of others.

Some lighthouse keepers filled the job for decades. In several cases, consecutive generations of the same family maintained a lighthouse. The introduction in the twentieth century of electricity, which could both provide the illumination and automatically control all the lighthouse's necessary functions, largely eliminated the need for resident keepers.

The twenty-one lighthouses sprinkled between Greenwich and Stonington are a motley group: tall and sleek, round and squat, rectangular and stony—even architecturally stylish. The oldest dates back to 1801; the newest was built in 1943.

The development in the latter half of the twentieth century of precise navigational charts, solar-powered signal buoys, and global positioning satellite technology rendered

New London Harbor Lighthouse, 1910–1939. Built in 1801, the New London Harbor Lighthouse is the oldest in Connecticut and the fourth oldest in the United States. At 80 feet, it is also the tallest lighthouse in Connecticut. The sleek, tapered eight-sided obelisk is the classic lighthouse silhouette.

Bridgeport Lighthouse, ca. 1893. Landlubbers often visited lighthouses to enjoy the vistas and the bracing maritime breeze. Usually they reached them by boat, but intensely cold weather could turn the waters of Long Island Sound into a solid pathway. This crowd of intrepid adventurers trekked across close to half a mile of ice to reach the Bridgeport Lighthouse, probably sometime in the early 1890s.

Built in 1871, the Bridgeport Lighthouse was actually fitted out with guns during the Spanish-American War in 1898, in case Spain decided to invade Connecticut. The lighthouse burned down in 1953.

New London Ledge Lighthouse, ca. 1910. It's no accident that the Southwest Ledge Light, also known as the New London Ledge Lighthouse, looks like a handsome home that somehow slid gracefully into the water and floated away. Local tradition says that the three-story lighthouse, made of red brick with white trim, was designed in the Second Empire style of architecture, complete with mansard roof, because residents of fine homes in New London and Groton didn't want their view of Long Island Sound marred by some aesthetically unpleasant structure.

Completed in 1909, this is one of three Connecticut lighthouses reported to be haunted. In this case, the ghost of a former lighthouse keeper, called "Ernie" for some unknown reason, is purportedly behind such spooky happenings as doors opening and closing by themselves and bedcovers being pulled down by invisible hands. The tale is that Ernie had an ugly romantic falling-out with either a girlfriend or his wife, depending upon which version is being told. Distraught, he climbed into the lighthouse tower, from which he plummeted to his death, either in a deliberate suicide jump, accidentally in a drunken stupor, or after slitting his throat.

many lighthouses obsolete. Although more than half of those along Connecticut's coast have been retained as active aids to navigation, others were removed from service. Some were allowed to fall into disrepair or even slated for demolition. Again and again public nostalgia and affection resulted in municipalities and preservation groups like the Faulkner's Light Brigade and the New London Maritime Society mounting campaigns to save and maintain these irreplaceable jewels in the crown of Connecticut's maritime heritage. Today, several Connecticut lighthouses have been converted to new uses, as nature preserve, parks, private residences, or museums.

16.
CLINTON

A crop-eared counterfeiter, cold cream, and Chardonnay are among the motley highlights of Clinton's past. And that's not all; the town's history also features a philanthropic transportation tycoon and an internationally acclaimed agronomist.

Clinton was settled in 1663 as part of Killingworth, which was incorporated as a town in 1667. Most of the early development in Killingworth took place in the southern part of town, near Long Island Sound, in what would become Clinton.

Clinton early found a place in history as the site of the first classes of Yale College. Founded in 1701, the Collegiate School, as Yale was originally called, was supposed to be located in Saybrook. But the new school's first—and for a time only—instructor, the Reverend Abraham Pierson, was pastor of the Congregational church in what today is Clinton. His parishioners refused to let him leave his pulpit to teach in Saybrook, with the result that the eighteen students who made up the first six years of Yale classes studied at Rev. Pierson's home in Clinton.

Yale's period in Clinton ended with Rev. Pierson's death in 1707. The origins in Clinton of the third college established in British North America are commemorated by a monument near the First Congregational Church indicating the approximate site where those first classes were held, and a statue of Rev. Abraham Pierson near the elementary school on East Main Street that bears his name.

Rev. Pierson was succeeded as Clinton's minister by one of those first Yalies, the Reverend Jared Eliot, who held the pastor's job for more than half a century. A trained physician as well, Rev. Eliot became the most respected and sought-after healer in New England.

Clinton's minister was also an energetic amateur scientist. He conducted experiments aimed at improving agriculture in New England and published his findings in works

Killingworth, Con.

Killingworth, ca. 1835

Clinton was on the verge of significant change when this sketch of what today is East Main Street, looking east near where it crosses the Indian River, was made in 1835. The Congregational meetinghouse in the middle, built in 1731, was torn down shortly thereafter, to be replaced in 1837 with the current church. The following year, the southern portion of Killingworth was incorporated as the town of Clinton.

By this time, about 150 houses had been built within a mile of the Congregational church. The ribs of a vessel under construction at one of the several shipyards on the Indian River can be seen down and to the left of the meetinghouse.

that became standard sources on farming techniques in the colonies. Another set of Rev. Eliot's experiments demonstrated that black sand that occasionally washed up on the Clinton beach was in fact iron ore that could be smelted into iron. Rev. Eliot published an account of his discovery, for which the small-town pastor from Connecticut was honored by the prestigious Royal Society of London for Improving Natural Knowledge.

Around the time of Eliot's death in 1763, another Clinton resident was applying his own remarkable talents to a less civic-minded pursuit. Abel Buell, born in Clinton in

Carter's Inn tavern sign, ca. 1823

Jared Carter pioneered the emergence of Clinton as a seaside getaway when he opened his inn on East Main Street in 1823. Carter intended his "Strangers' Resort" as not just a place for travelers passing through to get a meal or spend the night before continuing their journey, but as something different and innovative: a place for visitors to stay a spell to rest, recreate, and recuperate. Carter emphasized that his new establishment was situated "about eighty rods [approximately a quarter of a mile] from the water, commands an extensive view of the sound, and will be a pleasant and healthful resort for valetudinarians [physically frail or ailing persons] who may wish the benefit of the sea air."

The imagery on the sign that hung in front of Carter's inn made clear that he sought to cater literally to the carriage trade: an elegantly dressed couple traveling in an expensive vehicle driven by a coachman. Like operators of shoreline resorts today, Carter knew that delicious dining was an important part of an establishment's appeal. He assured prospective customers of his intention of "keeping on hand a constant supply of sea food."

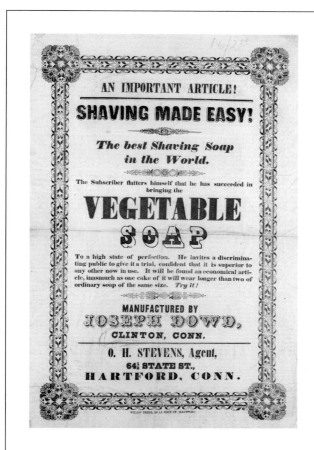

Vegetable soap manufactured by Joseph Dowd, 1846–1847

Clinton farmer Joseph Dowd displayed an entrepreneurial streak when he turned his hand to making and marketing vegetable soap in the mid-nineteenth century. Dowd may have been motivated to branch out beyond farming to produce what he claimed was the "best Shaving Soap in the World" by the need to support a rapidly growing family, which by 1850 included eight children, the eldest eighteen. The manufacture of personal grooming products would become a major industry in Clinton with the arrival in town of Pond's in 1888.

1742, had recently completed his training as a silversmith and opened a shop in his hometown. Buell proceeded to apply his skill to altering Connecticut paper currency, changing five-shilling bills into ones worth five pounds—thus increasing their value twentyfold.

Buell was caught and convicted of counterfeiting, a crime of which colonial authorities took an exceedingly dim view. His punishment included being branded on the forehead, the cropping of the bottom of one ear (he was reportedly allowed to affix the severed piece, which subsequently grew and reattached), and a jail sentence.

After being released from jail, Buell worked as a copperplate engraver. In 1784 he produced a milestone in cartography that is his chief claim to fame: the first map of the new United States, as established by the 1783 treaty that ended the Revolution, made by an American.

Buell spent the rest of his life pursuing a hodgepodge of ventures, from quarrying marble to manufacturing cotton. None proved profitable, and he died in the New Haven Alms House at the age of eighty-one.

MORGAN SCHOOL.
AND PRINCIPAL'S RESIDENCE.

More conventional Clinton residents farmed for a living or worked at shipbuilding, which was a major industry in Clinton from the early 1700s until the Civil War. Over the course of that century and a half, the town's shipyards turned out hundreds of vessels. Oystering also became an important economic activity in the early 1800s.

Clinton became a town separate from Killingworth in 1838. It was named in honor of New York governor DeWitt Clinton, the visionary who promoted construction of the Erie Canal between Buffalo and Albany, New York. At the time of Clinton's incorporation,

Morgan School, 1881

Charles Morgan was a fourteen-year-old farm boy when he left Clinton in 1819 to pursue a life path that would culminate in the building of a transportation empire of shipping lines and railroads in the Southern states. But the wealthy and successful Morgan never forgot the small shoreline town of his youth. Morgan gave $60,000 for construction in Clinton of a free public school, and another $50,000 toward its support. Dedicated in 1871, the Morgan School, as it was called in honor of its benefactor, included elementary through high school classes, with a student body of more than two hundred. Morgan's generosity toward the school that bore his name continued for the rest of his life. By the time he died in 1878, he had donated a total of more than $300,000—the equivalent of more than $6 million in twenty-first-century dollars—to the Morgan School, shown here in a detail from an 1881 bird's-eye view of Clinton. Clinton's modern Morgan High School is a direct descendant of the Morgan School, making it one of the oldest high schools in the state.

its population numbered around 1,200. That number would fluctuate, but never increase significantly, for the next century.

As early as the 1830s, Clinton was noted for its "salubrious sea air" during the summer. Following the Civil War, the town became a popular destination for warm-weather vacationers who arrived via road, railroad, or steamboat.

In 1888 there arrived in Clinton a new firm that remains an important part of the town's economy to this day. The T. T. Pond Company, which had been established by Theron

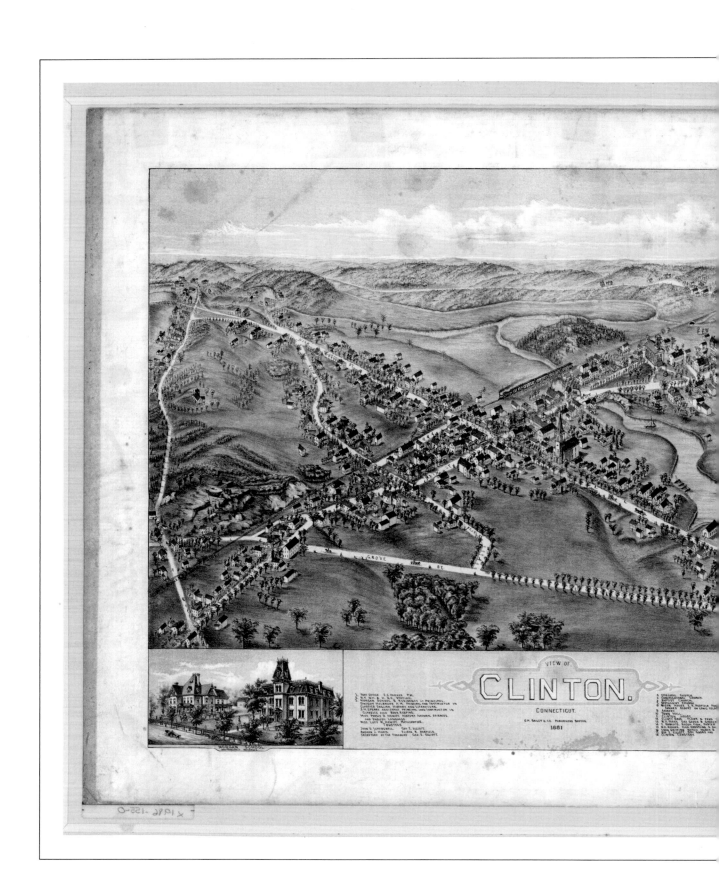

View of Clinton, Connecticut, 1881

Clinton's population increased by little more than 10 percent between 1835 and 1881, the year this bird's-eye view was published. Industrialization and massive immigration had all but bypassed the town, but there had been some important changes. The railroad now ran through town on tracks laid perilously close to the rear of the Congregational meetinghouse constructed in 1837. The Morgan School had been dedicated in 1871, and a monument had been erected to mark the site of Yale's first classes. Innkeeper Jared Clark's vision of Clinton as a destination for visitors looking to enjoy the delights of the shore had been vindicated, as evidenced by the Bacon House, the self-proclaimed "most popular summer resort on the Sound."

T. Pond in New York in 1849, removed fluid from the witch hazel plant to make a medicine called Pond's Extract, used to treat cuts and other afflictions. In 1907 the firm diversified into skin care products, introducing Pond's Cold Cream and Pond's Vanishing Cream. By the 1920s, Pond's was the nation's leading manufacturer of skin cream, and the company's products would eventually be sold to a global market.

Pond's expanded its product line in subsequent decades to include cosmetics. In 1955 Pond's merged with Chesebrough Manufacturing Company, originally established by Robert Chesebrough, the inventor of Vaseline, to create Chesebrough-Ponds. In 1987, almost exactly a century after Pond's first came to Clinton, Chesebrough-Ponds was acquired by the international firm Unilever, which today is the town's largest employer.

Like every shoreline town, phenomenal changes in population and transportation transformed Clinton radically during the second half of the twentieth century. The post–World War II baby boom, combined with the construction during the 1950s of the Connecticut Turnpike (modern Interstate 95), made Clinton a convenient and attractive place for people who worked in communities like New Haven, Old Saybrook, and other shoreline towns to buy a home and raise a family.

As a result, a population that for a century had grown little if at all abruptly increased from 2,466 in 1950 to 4,166 in 1960, then more than doubled to 10,267 by 1970. Between 1970 and 2000, growth was slower, but Clinton's population still increased by a third, to its current size of approximately 13,000. During the summer, vacationers seeking to enjoy the town's salt water, sand, and "salubrious sea air" cause the town's population to temporarily double.

17

WESTBROOK

*M*odern Westbrook was settled in the 1660s as part of Saybrook. Its two rivers, the Patchogue and the Menunketesuc, combined with the nearness of thick stands of white oak and chestnut, made shipbuilding the logical livelihood for many generations.

Construction of vessels including brigs, schooners, and sloops was big business in Westbrook from the 1700s into the early decades of the nineteenth century. Most shipyards were on the Patchogue, with at least one on the Menunketesuc.

At times shipbuilding seems to have risen to the level of a craze. "Almost any place was extemporized for a ship yard, numbers being built by the side of the highways and on the sound beach," according to nineteenth-century local historian James Pratt. "In the palmy days of the business, vessels were in process of construction continually, as many as a half dozen being on the stocks at once." Westbrook men also sailed the ships produced by the shipyards.

The industry that had sustained the town for a century went into decline around the time Westbrook was incorporated as a separate town in 1840. Shipbuilding became centralized in cities, resulting in the shutdown of yards in small towns like Westbrook. But enterprising Westbrook residents found another way to derive a living from the rivers and the sea. Shad, although notoriously bony, had always been plentiful along the immediate shoreline and even in the rivers—so plentiful that in the early 1800s, according to historian Pratt, "to offer it to a guest at dinner was considered an evidence of excessive economy and almost a disgrace." But as shad gradually became less abundant, it turned, according to Pratt, into a "marketable fish, and finally a luxury." Westbrook men went to work catching the once-scorned, now valuable fish, at first using large nets or "seines."

Shad fishing became one of Westbrook's major industries with the introduction in 1849 of "pound fishing"—a practice that involved stretching nets between poles anchored

Northwest view of Westbrook, ca. 1835

Westbrook was a flourishing community in Saybrook, soon to become a separate town when this drawing of the village center was made in 1835. The view looks southeast, from a spot on the west side of the Patchogue River, toward the handsome new Congregational meetinghouse, built in 1829 on the Boston Post Road site where the First Congregational Church stands today.

Shipbuilding on the Patchogue River, which had begun a century earlier, was still a thriving industry. The vessel in the picture may have been a new one just off the ways or one of the fifteen vessels owned by Westbrook residents that engaged in trade with towns along the Atlantic coast.

at a distance offshore. Fishermen would harvest the fish that were snagged in the nets several times a day. By the 1880s, five or six dozen Westbrook fishermen were hauling in a total of one hundred thousand shad a year.

Circumstances were looking brighter for Westbrook residents on another front, as the town became one of Connecticut's earliest beach resorts in the 1870s.

"The unsurpassed fishing and bathing of its bay have drawn to Westbrook a new population, which, during the summer months, nearly doubles its census," James Pratt

Old Kirtland homestead overlooking Long Island Sound, ca. 1900–1929

Westbrook's population of 1,200 in 1850 had declined by a quarter, to about nine hundred, in 1880. "The fact that shipbuilding, which was once of consequence, both to the builder and to the timber men, has disappeared, that farming has ceased to be a profitable occupation, and that manufacturing never existed to any considerable extent, may account for it somewhat," theorized local historian James Pratt. Many natives of the town, particularly young people, had been forced to leave Westbrook, and indeed Connecticut, to find fresh opportunities far from home.

A case in point is the Kirtland family, who occupied this homestead for several generations. Nathan Kirtland's ancestors had lived in Westbrook since the 1600s. In 1777, when Nathan was just sixteen, he enlisted in the fight for American independence and spent more than a year guarding the shoreline from New London to Guilford.

Nathan had one son, Philip, born in 1799, and it was likely that providing for him wasn't a problem, even in the lean decades of the early 1800s in Connecticut. Philip, however, fathered seven sons who survived to manhood, and all of them could not possibly hope to make a good living in Westbrook, or even in Connecticut. Philip's youngest son remained in Westbrook, but his six elder brothers left Connecticut, finding work as fishermen, sailors, and merchants hundreds of miles from home. Four of them ultimately settled in Wisconsin, and another in Massachusetts. The sixth son spent time in Michigan but eventually returned home to Westbrook to work as a fisherman.

Westbrook, 1870s

Going to the seashore in the 1870s required clothes not much different than those worn on the street, as the people on this Westbrook beach demonstrate. However, the full dress didn't prohibit sitting on the sand, or even, at least in the case of the two women next to the rowboat on the far right, wading ankle-deep into the water. The poles with what appear to be nets strung between them extending far out into the water may be an example of the "pound fishing" that was a lucrative industry in Westport for decades during the nineteenth century.

noted in 1884. "The sound front is being rapidly covered with cottages, which now number about 100"—an impressive number for a town with barely nine hundred year-round residents.

More than a century later, with the town's population approaching seven thousand, summer vacationers remain a staple of Westbrook's economy. Two-thirds of the businesses in town are in either the trade or service industry, many of them providing lodging, dining, and shopping amenities for those drawn to Westbrook's beaches.

Salt Meadow

Esther Lape, a writer and activist who numbered being one of the founders of the League of Women Voters among her many accomplishments, and Elizabeth Read, an attorney, together owned more than 150 acres on Long Island Sound in Westbrook that they called Salt Meadow. On the property they built a log house, constructed of trees toppled by the Great Hurricane of 1938, to serve as a rustic getaway from their professional and political pursuits.

A frequent guest at Salt Meadow was Lape and Read's close friend, First Lady Eleanor Roosevelt. During her twelve years in the White House, and for fifteen years, Mrs. Roosevelt crusaded for many causes, including equal rights for women and African Americans, relief for the millions of Americans suffering from the effects of the Great Depression, and aid to refugees from the devastation of World War II.

One of Mrs. Roosevelt's influential tools was the nationally syndicated newspaper column "My Day," which she wrote six days a week from 1935 until 1962. She penned a number of articles while staying at the Salt Meadow cabin, where she enjoyed the natural surroundings. Her column for February 28, 1950, described a snowy morning at Salt Meadow: "The sky was blue and the day was really wonderful. As we walked quietly along Miss Lape stopped suddenly and pointed ahead. There, bounding through the woods, was a doe with her white tail high—the most graceful sight I have seen in many a long day."

Esther Lape gave the property to the U.S. Fish and Wildlife Service in 1972. It was the original piece of what is today the Stewart B. McKinney National Wildlife Refuge. Today's 274 acres of the Salt Meadow Unit provide habitat for birds that include great egrets, glossy ibis, bluebirds, and red-tailed hawks, and for other animals such as red fox and coyotes.

Cottages, ca. 1870s

Vacationers pose in front of two of the dozens of cottages that were built along Westbrook's shoreline in the 1870s.

Happy Fourth of July, 1889

By 1889, beachwear had become less cumbersome, although it still modestly covered most of the body, as these eight young members of the Steele and Annis families perched on a rowboat at a Westbrook beach on the Fourth of July show.

Wooden Submarine

In 1775, Westbrook native David Bushnell invented history's first working manned submarine. Bushnell created the vessel, an advanced piece of technology for its time, as a "secret weapon" to help win America's war for independence.

Born in Westbrook in 1740, David Bushnell spent the first thirty years of his life working the family farm. In 1771 he at last was able to afford to enroll at Yale, graduating in 1775.

Bushnell had an inventive talent that he put to use while still at Yale. At a secluded spot on the Connecticut River in Old Saybrook, he invented and built, with his brother Ezra's help, a one-man submarine. The vessel was about seven feet high and three and a half feet across. It consisted of two large pieces of oak held tightly together by iron bands and made waterproof by a coating of tar. It was called the *Turtle,* from its resemblance to two turtle shells fastened together.

The *Turtle* could hold just one man, who did everything. He powered and maneuvered the submarine by manually cranking propellers, made it submerge and surface by using his foot on a pedal that let water into a chamber or expelled it, navigated, and carried out the attack. This last function involved sneaking up on an enemy ship at night, then submerging under its hull. The operator would screw an auger, positioned atop the *Turtle* and attached to a 150-pound keg of gunpowder, into the target's hull. When the *Turtle* detached itself from the auger, leaving it buried in the ship's hull, the bomb was automatically armed. The *Turtle*'s operator had twenty minutes to make a getaway before the gunpowder exploded and, it was hoped, blew a hole in the enemy ship's hull that would severely damage or, ideally, sink it.

The *Turtle* first went into action on the night of September 6, 1776, its target the flagship of the massive British fleet anchored in New York Harbor. The operator was an eleventh-hour replacement for the *Turtle*'s usual crewman, David Bushnell's brother Ezra, who had fallen ill. All went as planned, until the operator tried to screw the auger into the ship's hull—and struck not wood, but metal. He was not strong or skilled enough to maneuver the *Turtle* to make a second try at inserting the auger and was forced to break off the mission.

The *Turtle* made two more attempts to attack British ships; both were unsuccessful. The world's first submarine was destroyed in a British bombardment a little more than a month after its first trial.

18.

OLD SAYBROOK

Sometimes one generation's obstacle is another generation's blessing. The sandbars at the mouth of the Connecticut River blocked sailing vessels over a certain size, prohibiting Old Saybrook from developing into the large city that otherwise almost certainly would have been its destiny. Thanks to that barrier that frustrated generations of traders and entrepreneurs, not just Old Saybrook but the lower Connecticut River Valley are today remarkably unspoiled, with only small towns along the banks.

Old Saybrook started out as an independent colony and a military fortification. In 1631 prominent English Puritans acquired the title to a large tract of land that included modern Old Saybrook, Lyme, Old Lyme, Westbrook, Deep River, Essex, Chester, East Lyme, and part of Waterford. They named their new colony Saybrook, after two of the group's members, Lord Say and Sele and Lord Brook. In 1635 they chose as governor John Winthrop Jr., who the next year arranged for the construction of a palisade fort as a defense against local Pequots and Dutch from New Amsterdam.

The second governor of Saybrook was George Fenwick, who brought with him from England to the wilderness fortification his young wife, Alice, and their infant son. In 1644 George Fenwick arranged the sale of the fort and the Saybrook Colony to the Connecticut Colony, headquartered in Hartford.

The fort at Saybrook burned down in 1647, and a new one was constructed near the site of the original. It protected the coast from attacks by Dutch and later, in the 1700s and early 1800s, by the enemy British, until it was razed in 1870.

Old Saybrook was supposed to be the site of Yale College, but that plan was sidetracked, then permanently scotched. The school's trustees met in Old Saybrook in 1701 and chose Rev. Abraham Pierson to be the first—and for a time only—teacher. Pierson was pastor of the Congregational church in Clinton, whose members refused

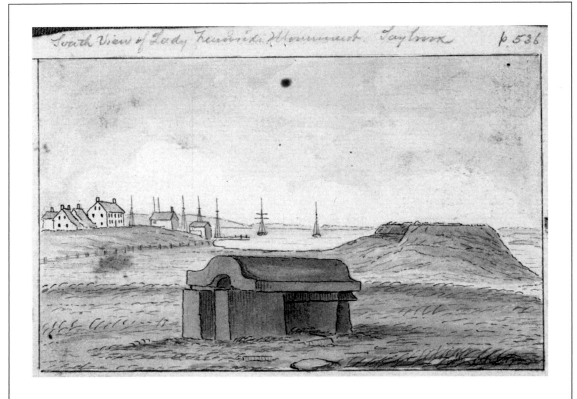

South View of Lady Fenwick's Monument, Saybrook. p.536

South view of Lady Fenwick's Monument, Saybrook, ca. 1835

Although Lady Alice Fenwick lived but a few years in Old Saybrook, this young mother has for centuries been a local icon. She came from England to the crude fort at Old Saybrook in 1639 with her second husband, Governor George Fenwick, and their infant son. She was known as "Lady" Fenwick because her first marriage to a knight gave her the right to that courtesy title.

Two daughters were born in Old Saybrook to Lady Fenwick, who is believed to have died not long after the birth of the second in 1645. She was buried on a hill inside Saybrook Fort, and over her grave was erected a "tablestone"—a massive slab of brownstone supported by three stone pillars that was at the time an expensive luxury.

George Fenwick returned to England with his motherless children and apparently never came back to Connecticut. Over the next two centuries Lady Fenwick's tomb became a fixture of Old Saybrook history, meriting inclusion in John Warner Barber's 1836 Connecticut Historical Collections.

In 1870 progress threatened to disturb the site where Lady Fenwick had lain for so long. Her grave lay in the path of the planned route of the Connecticut Valley Railroad, but Lady Fenwick was rescued from the advance of the iron horse. Her grave was opened, revealing bones "in a good state of preservation" and "a braid of auburn hair." The remains were reinterred in Cypress Cemetery about a quarter of a mile away, and the original massive monument was placed over her new resting place. After a few years, an iron fence was erected around the monument to discourage people from chipping off bits of it as souvenirs.

James Pharmacy, ca. 1945

The James Pharmacy, built in 1790 as a general store, has several varied claims to fame. The first occurred in 1824, when Revolutionary War hero the Marquis de Lafayette stopped here to shop during a triumphant nostalgia tour of the nation he had helped to achieve independence nearly half a century earlier

The building was moved to its current site in 1877. In 1902 Peter Lane, who in 1895 had become one of the first two African Americans to earn a pharmacy degree in Connecticut, turned it into a drug store. In 1917 the store was taken over by Lane's sister-in-law, Anna Louise James, a 1908 graduate of the Brooklyn College of Pharmacy, who was the first African-American woman in Connecticut to become a pharmacist. For the next fifty years she operated the James Pharmacy and Soda Fountain, which became a childhood fixture for generations of Old Saybrook residents.

Peter Lane's daughter Ann also earned a pharmacy degree and worked in the James Pharmacy with her aunt Anna Louise. Ann went on to become an acclaimed novelist under her married name of Ann Petry.

Anna Louise James died in 1977, and the building stood vacant for several years. The James Pharmacy and Soda Fountain was restored and reopened in 1984.

Fenwick Hall, ca. 1871

Share owners in the New Saybrook Company included construction of a luxurious resort hotel in the plans for their summer community. Fenwick Hall, photographed around the time it opened for business in 1871, was situated and designed for guests' maximum comfort and pleasure. Its location on Saybrook Point offered spectacular views as far as Long Island and Fishers Island. The architect's layout allowed the breeze off Long Island Sound to freshen just about every one of the more than 150 guest rooms. Fenwick Hall didn't prove financially successful in the long run, and the building burned down in 1917.

Leverett Brainard cottage, Fenwick, 1890s

Fenwick Hall is in the background on the right, and the cottage of Leverett Brainard is on the far left in this photograph of Fenwick taken in the 1890s. Two of the three girls are Brainard's daughters Edith and Ruth. The boy in the photograph is Morgan G. Bulkeley Jr. Leverett Brainard's wife was Morgan Bulkeley Sr.'s sister, making Edith, Ruth, and Morgan Jr. cousins.

to let him relocate to Old Saybrook. As a result, Yale's classes were held in Clinton until Rev. Pierson's death in 1707. Old Saybrook had to settle for hosting each year's commencement.

Upon Rev. Pierson's death, the senior class moved to Milford, while the underclassmen relocated to Old Saybrook. This inconvenient arrangement got even worse in 1716, when students were scattered among Hartford, Wethersfield, Old Saybrook, and Madison. Commencements, however, were still held at Old Saybrook.

A movement arose to construct a building specifically to house the college and thereby settle once and for all its location. Residents of Hartford, Wethersfield, and Old Saybrook pledged substantial sums of money toward the college if it were to be built in their town, but all were outbid by New Haven.

Aetna Outing, Fenwick Hall, ca. 1900

Fenwick was a summer outpost of Hartford's Aetna Life Insurance Company, as this photograph of a company outing taken around 1900 at Fenwick Hall demonstrates. The man in the middle is Morgan Bulkeley, president of Aetna from 1879 until his death in 1922. On the left in the picture is Joel L. English, vice president of Aetna, and to the right is Ferdinand A. Hart, Aetna's agent for Massachusetts.

Morgan Bulkeley was also a major figure in Connecticut politics for three decades. He served as mayor of Hartford from 1880 to 1888, governor of Connecticut from 1890 to 1893, and U.S. senator from Connecticut from 1905 to 1911.

In 1717 New Haven hosted the commencement of the college, and the next year the school's new building in New Haven was ready. It was named Yale after a merchant who made a large donation of goods and books. Old Saybrook residents, however, refused to relinquish their claim to the college without one final fight.

The governor and his advisers met in Old Saybrook and issued a warrant to the sheriff allowing him to take possession of books belonging to the Yale library that remained in Old Saybrook. The sheriff had to force his way through an unhappy crowd to get to the building in which the books were stored, and the carts to carry the volumes to New Haven were vandalized. When the transfer finally got under way, it was hampered by the sabotage of bridges on the road to New Haven. Once the library reached New Haven, it was discovered that about 250 books were missing. They were never recovered.

In the mid-1700s a brisk trade with the West Indies, mostly conducted in small ships, emerged as an important factor in Old Saybrook's economy. But for more than a century following the American Revolution, harvesting the bounty of the sea right from the shore proved an even more lucrative and long-lasting livelihood for hundreds of Old Saybrook residents.

Every spring for more than 250 years, shad returned from the sea in enormous numbers to swim up the Connecticut River to their spawning grounds. "Connecticut river shad are considered superior to any other in this country," claimed local historian John Warner Barber in 1836. The fish were caught with varying kinds of nets extended out from shore into the waters of Long Island Sound. At times a single pull on a net could haul in thousands of shad, which were usually salted and shipped to markets in cities such as Hartford and New York.

The original Saybrook Colony had begun shrinking in 1665, when the area comprising the modern towns of Lyme, East Lyme, Old Lyme, and part of Waterford separated from it. Chester became an independent town in 1836, as did Westbrook in 1840. Old Saybrook was incorporated as a town in 1852. It still included the modern town of Essex, which broke off in 1854, leaving Old Saybrook with its current boundaries. Two centuries after its establishment, the once-extensive Saybrook Colony now consisted of what today is the modern town of Deep River, the name chosen in 1947 to replace Saybrook to avoid confusion with Old Saybrook.

Another water-related pursuit besides fishing was catching on in Old Saybrook before the Civil War: vacationing. The town became home to what is one of the most prestigious summer colonies in America as a result of a project undertaken by a group of wealthy and well-connected Hartford residents in 1870.

The section known as "Lynde Farm" or "Light House Point" was undeveloped land along Long Island Sound. Its appeal as a site for a summer colony was increased by the

Riverside Rowing Club, ca. 1890–1909

More lounging than paddling seems to be taking place at the floating dock of the Riverside Rowing Club off Fenwick around the turn of the twentieth century.

construction of the Connecticut Valley Railroad, completed in 1871 between Hartford and Old Saybrook, which made traveling between city and shore quick and convenient.

In 1870 the land was purchased by the New Saybrook Company, a joint stock company created so that, in the euphemistic phrasing of William B. Tully, writing in 1884, "the stockholders should be gentlemen well esteemed in their respective communities, and that there should be none likely to disturb the harmony which should exist in a large company gathered for a few months in the summer for purposes of health and recreation." Every one of the original seventy stockholders, each of whom owned $1,000 worth of shares, was entitled to a half-acre lot. A total of 130 lots were ultimately sold.

By 1884, eighteen cottages had been constructed at what was now called Fenwick. Today Fenwick is a separate borough of Old Saybrook, with a permanent population of fewer than one hundred, some descended from the founding New Saybrook Company shareholders.

Without significant industry to attract large numbers of immigrants, and the eventual decline in fishing and maritime trade, Old Saybrook's population grew at a glacial pace during the first century after its incorporation as a town. It started with 1,105 people in 1860 and didn't rise above 2,000 until 1950. The post–World War II baby boom and suburbanization finally jump-started population growth in Old Saybrook. The number of residents quadrupled to 10,367 in 2000.

19.
OLD LYME

*N*ature and art, intertwined for more than a century, have made Old Lyme a town unlike any other on the Connecticut coast. At the turn of the twentieth century, its pastoral landscape inspired a band of painters pioneering a new, distinctively American style of art. In their wake came a naturalist whose talent for painting the birds he loved introduced millions to the joys of ornithology, and whose activities in Old Lyme helped launch the modern environmental movement. Yet another Old Lyme artist with a passion for everything nuts (the edible kind) became a minor celebrity of American pop culture.

Nature's practical aspects—the productivity of the land and the proximity of the sea that for centuries was the most efficient highway—shaped Old Lyme's first 250 years. Settled in 1664, what today is Old Lyme was originally part of the town of Lyme, which was incorporated in 1667.

Old Lyme developed along the Lieutenant River, which flows into the Connecticut River not far from where it joins Long Island Sound. Maritime trade with the West Indies, involving the export of lumber, livestock, and meat from the region's farms, was a thriving enterprise from the early 1700s until after the American Revolution.

In 1775 secret tests of the first submarine, the invention of David Bushnell of Westbrook, Connecticut, were conducted in the Connecticut River off Old Lyme. Sgt. Ezra Lee of Old Lyme piloted the one-man wooden vessel, called the *Turtle* for its resemblance to that amphibian, on its first mission against the enemy in New York Harbor in 1776.

Following the Revolution, building of conventional ships emerged as an important industry in Old Lyme. Between 1784 and 1888, two hundred vessels were constructed in town. Old Lyme men and boys served as captains and crew on many of these ships, which sailed as far as Antarctica.

West view of Lyme, Con

West view of Lyme, ca. 1835

The First Congregational Church's house of worship has dominated the center of Old Lyme for nearly two centuries. The meetinghouse seen in this view of "the Street," as the main avenue through town was simply called, looking east across the Lieutenant River around 1835, was built in 1816–1817 by Col. Samuel Belcher. It burned down in 1907 and was replaced in 1910 by a building that replicated its predecessor as closely as possible.

In 1855, what today makes up Old Lyme was incorporated as a separate town called South Lyme. In 1857 the name was changed to Old Lyme, perhaps in imitation of Old Saybrook, with the idea that *old* carried with it a certain cachet.

During the second half of the nineteenth century, a surge of industrialization and urbanization rapidly transformed the face of America. The massive influx of immigrants, the grit and grime of factories, the noise and congestion of cities that accompanied these developments unsettled many Americans, still recovering from a horrendous Civil War. There arose a yearning for a simpler, more tranquil existence lived close to the nurturing, reassuring stability of nature.

South view of Gov. Griswold's house in Lyme ca. 1835

South view of Gov. Griswold's house in Lyme, ca. 1835

Dynasties were common in Connecticut politics and government from the beginning. Black Hall in Old Lyme is closely associated with one family whose power and prominence spanned more than six decades.

Black Hall was built in 1810, on land that had belonged to the Griswold family since the mid-1600s, by Roger Griswold, who the next year was elected governor of Connecticut. Roger Griswold's father, Matthew Griswold, had served as governor of Connecticut from 1784 to 1786. Roger's maternal grandfather, Roger Wolcott, had been governor from 1750 to 1754.

Roger Griswold died in office in 1812. The house he built just before being elevated to the state's top job still stands, a reminder of a time when family ties were an important factor in determining who occupied the most powerful political offices.

That longing was responded to by a group of American artists who adopted a new style of painting, termed Impressionism, that had emerged in recent decades in France. Impressionism derived its name from the goal of producing a painting that captured the artist's perception or impression of the subject, usually something from everyday life, rather than depicting it as precisely and literally as possible. Many American Impressionists found the serenity, the tranquility, the bucolic beauty of the preindustrial America they sought to paint in Old Lyme, described by a travel writer in 1926 as "perhaps the most peaceful, lovely old town in the Connecticut Valley."

Old Lyme's destiny to become one of the biggest and most important American art colonies of the early twentieth century was assured by the very practical need for Miss Florence Griswold to operate her large, handsome family home as a boardinghouse. Miss Griswold, a well-educated and cultured middle-aged maiden lady, had fallen upon hard times as the result of a series of family and financial misfortunes. To support herself, she rented rooms in her house.

Shopping scene at Sound View, ca. 1911

Women and children are clustered around a shopping cart at Sound View around 1911. The horse-drawn wagon was a convenient mobile sales outlet that offered food, clothing, and household goods to locals or vacationers enjoying the popular beach and waters of Long Island Sound.

Summer visitors still flock to Old Lyme. In season the town's year-round population of eight thousand nearly doubles.

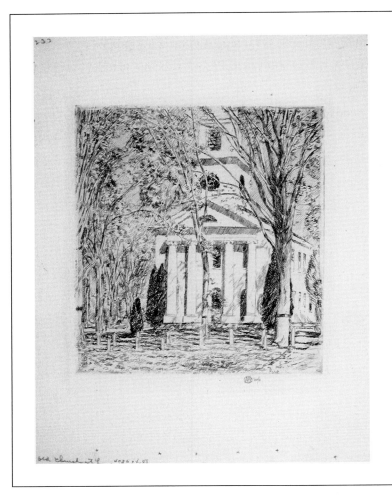

The church at Old Lyme, 1924

The First Congregational Church in Old Lyme, built in 1817, was a popular subject for visiting summer artists. Childe Hassam, one of the best-known American Impressionists, produced paintings and drawings of the building, as well as etchings like this one done in 1924.

The first artist lodged at Florence Griswold's boardinghouse in 1899. Word spread quickly of the pastoral, unspoiled atmosphere of Old Lyme. In 1903 Childe Hassam, a leading light of American Impressionism, came to stay and paint, and more and more artists flocked to Old Lyme, eventually numbering in the dozens. Over the next two decades, Florence Griswold's boardinghouse and twelve acres on the Lieutenant River became the headquarters of the Old Lyme Impressionist colony.

"Miss Florence," as she was affectionately known, served as a kind of housemother to a refined fraternity/sorority house. Many artists brought their wives with them, and a couple of female painters lodged at the house. The artists insisted that they had to approve any new guests.

The painters Miss Florence termed "her boys" showed up each spring with all their luggage and equipment for a several months' stay during which they spent their days outside, painting Old Lyme's fields and marshes; its woods and flowers; its historic buildings, rustic barns, bridges, and roads; and its riverbanks and seashore. Miss Florence handled their rooming arrangements, served three meals a day, and accommodated their working needs by such services as transforming small buildings on her property into studios and maintaining small boats for them to use to paint water scenes. Her hospitality, as well as her encouragement and support, created a communal atmosphere in which the artists could work with the greatest creativity.

Old Lyme's profile as a center of art got a boost in 1902, when artists began holding an annual summer exhibition of their work in the local library. Trains and boats delivered flocks of art enthusiasts to the exhibition, which was reviewed in publications across the country. Some artists purchased houses and made Old Lyme their year-round home. Impressionist paintings of Old Lyme were included in international exhibitions. The Lyme Art Association formed in 1914, and in 1921 it opened a gallery managed by Florence Griswold.

Old Lyme's heyday as an art colony was coming to an end by the mid-1920s. Florence Griswold sold the house in 1936 and died the following year. The Florence Griswold Association bought the house in 1941, and in 1947 it opened it as the Florence Griswold Museum. The house was designated a National Historical Landmark in 1993.

An artist who appreciated and painted nature in a different manner and for a different purpose arrived in Old Lyme in 1954. Roger Tory Peterson was already renowned as the author and illustrator of the pioneering *A Field Guide to the Birds,* first published in 1934. Peterson painted the birds he had loved since boyhood, then described them in a guidebook that turned millions of people into bird-watchers.

Peterson sought in Old Lyme what the Impressionists had, an undeveloped place in which he could observe and paint nature. But what he observed turned him into a crusader to save the nature he loved. During the 1950s and 1960s, Peterson noticed that the number of ospreys in Old Lyme had declined alarmingly. Scientists determined that the pesticide DDT, ingested by the birds via the fish they ate, caused the shells of the osprey eggs to be so thin and fragile that they broke before the chick inside could develop. Peterson's observations and activism contributed to the United States' decision in 1972 to ban DDT.

Peterson died in 1996. Four years later, 588 acres at the mouth of the Connecticut River, where Peterson had often spent time watching birds, were dedicated as the Roger Tory Peterson Wildlife Area at Great Island.

Yet another artistic style and subject from nature were the focus of a painter who was a bit more eccentric than others who had worked in Old Lyme. Elizabeth Tashjian was a graduate of the prestigious National Academy of Design. During her time at the academy, she began turning out paintings of nuts, which she had enjoyed both as edibles and playthings as a child.

Tashjian and her mother purchased a large Victorian house in Old Lyme in 1950, and Tashjian became involved in the Lyme Art Association. After her mother's death in 1959, Tashjian withdrew into herself for a time. Then in 1972, on an impulse, she opened

"MISS FLORENCE" IN HER DINING ROOM.

Miss Florence Griswold in her dining room, ca. 1915

Florence Griswold's hospitality and support led artists of Old Lyme's American Impressionist colony to deem her boardinghouse "Holy House." In an expression of gratitude, they executed more than forty paintings on the interior walls and doors of the house. Miss Florence is depicted sitting in front of several of those works in her dining room, sometime around 1915.

the first floor of her home as the Nut Museum, in which she displayed her paintings and sculptures, walnut jewelry, a Nativity scene made of nuts, and actual nuts, including a thirty-five-pound coco-de-mer, an example of the world's largest nut. People donated nuts to her collection, and she wrote songs about nuts.

The tiny Tashjian—she was just four feet tall—attracted the national spotlight for her unusual passion. She appeared on the *Tonight Show* with Johnny Carson and was the subject of newspaper and magazine articles, as well as a documentary film. Travel guidebooks highlighted the Nut Museum, which charged $3 and a nut for admission.

In 2002, Tashjian, ninety, fell ill, and the Nut Museum closed. She died in 2007.

Although best known as a colorful character, late in life Tashjian was recognized as a "visionary avant-garde" artist. Her paintings, her nut collection, and her papers are preserved by Connecticut College's Program in Museum Studies. The Lyman Allyn Art Museum in New London mounted a display of her work in 2004.

Art continues to flourish in Old Lyme. Nearly a century after its founding, the Lyme Art Association continues to sponsor classes, exhibitions, and sales. The Lyme Academy College of Fine Arts, founded in 1976, offers degree programs. The Florence Griswold Museum has expanded into a complex that includes the house, restored gardens, an education center, artist William Chadwick's studio, and the innovatively designed Robert and Nancy Krieble Gallery. The museum's holdings were also greatly enriched by the donation of the Hartford Steam Boiler Inspection and Insurance Company's collection of nearly two hundred works of American art.

20

EAST LYME

Settlement of the area that today makes up East Lyme began in the 1640s. For the first two centuries, growth centered in the northern part of town, called Flanders. That began to change around the time East Lyme was incorporated as a separate town in 1839, cobbled together from a piece of Old Lyme on the west and of Waterford on the east. Several developments sparked an economic and population boom in the shoreline portion of town, called Niantic, which up to this time had been sparsely settled.

The first was the emergence of ocean fishing as an important industry. An estimated fifty ships sailed from East Lyme for the Georges Bank fishing grounds in the Atlantic Ocean off the coast of Cape Cod to catch cod and halibut. The thriving fishing industry spawned related economic activities in Niantic, including shipbuilding on the banks of the Niantic River and retail firms selling supplies.

The second was construction of the first railroad line to Niantic in 1852. Raw materials and finished goods could now be shipped conveniently and economically. In addition, Niantic Bay became easily accessible by train for city dwellers looking for summer vacation spots. Cottages began to go up, along with hotels and restaurants.

Small granite quarries also opened in Niantic in the middle of the nineteenth century. They produced pink stone for buildings and monuments for the next hundred years.

Many residents of Flanders moved south to bustling Niantic like sand running to the bottom of an hourglass. Immigrants increased the town's population as well.

East Lyme fell into a slump beginning in the 1880s. Georges Bank was fished so heavily that first halibut, then cod, nearly disappeared from its waters. Local businesses that depended upon the fishing fleet also declined.

In 1881 the Connecticut National Guard established in Niantic a training facility that exists to this day. Since at least the early twentieth century, the camp has borne the

Keeping the Inn in the Family

In 1790 "a kick of a horse in his bowels" killed Dr. Daniel Caulkins, who left behind a widow and eleven children. For the next twenty-seven years Elizabeth Caulkins supported herself and her large family by running the inn in Flanders that her husband had operated since 1781.

Managing an inn or tavern was one of the very few ways in which a woman could make a living two centuries ago. The work took place at home—literally—and required expertise at skills that a housewife would have mastered: cooking, cleaning, laundry.

In 1817 the Widow Caulkins's youngest son, Elisha, born just the year before his father died, took over running the inn from his mother, who was nearing seventy. Elisha continued to operate it for many more years.

name of the sitting governor. In recent years it has been Camp Grasso, Camp O'Neill, Camp Weicker, and Camp Rowland. Legislation that would have given the facility the permanent name of Camp Ribicoff, for Connecticut governor and U.S. senator Abraham Ribicoff—thus eliminating the expense of changing signs and other materials every time a new governor took office—was introduced into the General Assembly in 2001 but failed to pass. And so, in 2009 the state's National Guardsmen train at Camp Rell.

East Lyme's population was 1,382 in 1850. The passage of a century saw the number of residents nearly triple, to 3,870. But then during just the next twenty years, between

**Bride Brook wedding float Connecticut Tercentenary Parade, Hartford,
October 12, 1935**

A legendary wedding from East Lyme's earliest years was re-created on a float for Connecticut's tercentenary parade in Hartford in October of 1935. The participants were descendants of those who took part in the original ceremony during the winter of 1646–1647.

Jonathan Rudd and Mary Metcalf of Saybrook, which then included Old Lyme and part of East Lyme, had made plans to be married, only to have a heavy snowstorm make it impossible for the magistrate who was to perform the wedding to reach them. Frustrated, the engaged couple turned for help to John Winthrop Jr., who had just settled in New London, which at that time included Waterford and part of East Lyme.

Winthrop held a commission from the Massachusetts Bay Colony that was recognized in New London, but it gave him no authority to conduct marriages in Saybrook. Rather than disappoint the eager-to-be newlyweds, Winthrop proposed a unique solution: Winthrop met Jonathan and Mary at a site on a stream called the Sunkipaug, which waterway Winthrop considered to be the boundary between Saybrook and New London. Winthrop united the couple in matrimony in a ceremony conducted on the eastern or New London side of the stream, which ever after has been known as Bride Brook.

The Thomas Lee House. East Lyme, Conn.

Thomas Lee House, ca. 1950

Thanks to what one historian termed "benign neglect" by generations of occupants, the Thomas Lee House in the southwestern portion of town, the original part of which dates from 1660, is a remarkably well-preserved example of a home from East Lyme's earliest days.

The house began as a two-room structure built around 1660 by Thomas Lee. Around 1690 Lee added two more rooms, doubling the house's size, probably to accommodate his dozen children.

A road constructed in 1715 ran behind the Lee House, leaving it facing away from the road. The house was expanded yet again with the addition of a lean-to on what had been its front, giving it the classic saltbox shape and also putting its front door on the road side.

The house remained in the Lee family for 250 years. In 1914 the East Lyme Historical Society purchased it and has operated it ever since as a museum. Each time the house had been enlarged or remodeled, the conservative, cost-conscious Lees had made no more alterations than absolutely necessary. That same less-is-more attitude was followed by pioneering architecture historian Norman Isham when he undertook a restoration for the East Lyme Historical Society.

Ye Church at East Lyme, ca. 1920s

Stone from East Lyme granite quarries was used to build the Congregational meetinghouse in Flanders around 1832. The congregation, established in 1719, had nearly died out by 1793, but the few remaining members regrouped and revitalized the church, leading to construction of its handsome new building.

The ascendance of Niantic as the center of life in East Lyme following the Civil War spelled the end of what had come to be called the Old Stone Church. The marble on the floor of the porch was sold in 1870 for money to keep the congregation going. A new church was built in Niantic, and in 1878 the stone building was auctioned off. It was torn down soon after. Its ruins were harvested for stone for various purposes, including a fireplace in the old Niantic Library.

"A sham battle," Connecticut National Guard, Niantic vicinity, July 1913

Connecticut National Guardsmen's rifles bristle between the openings in a rail fence, behind which they formed up as part of the mock combat maneuvers that were a highlight of the guardsmen's six-day-long annual tour of duty, headquartered at Camp Baldwin in Niantic, in July of 1913.

1950 and 1970, the town's population nearly tripled, to 11,399. The causes were several, including the post–World War II baby boom; construction of the Connecticut Turnpike, which made commuting to employment centers such as Groton and New London convenient; and the movement of families from cities into new suburban neighborhoods.

East Lyme's population grew by another 50 percent between 1970 and 2000, to 18,118. The population balance began to shift in favor of Flanders, where large areas of land were developed for housing and commercial uses. During the summer, vacationers who flock to Niantic for its public and private beaches, and for boating and sport fishing, swell the population to twice its year-round size.

2d Reg. Doing "Tango"...Waiting at depot for other Companies, July 1913

Soldiers of the Connecticut National Guard Second Regiment waiting for the arrival of a troop train carrying other guardsmen on the first day of the 1913 annual tour of duty at Camp Baldwin pass the time with a bit of silliness: dancing the tango, the hot new dance sweeping America, to music supplied by the unit's band.

COASTAL WEATHER

Severe weather has always been an inevitable, but unpredictable, factor of life along the Connecticut coast. Hurricanes have ripped apart shoreline towns, while snowstorms have buried them.

Winter Storms

One of the heaviest snowfalls ever recorded in Connecticut occurred in 1717. Called simply the Great Snow, it actually consisted of a series of four storms that occurred between February 27 and March 7. As much as five feet of snow fell, with drifts up to twenty-five feet tall. Some people, unable to open their houses' snow-blocked doors, strapped on snowshoes and stepped right out of their second-floor windows onto the piled-up white stuff.

There were no reports of people losing their lives in the Great Snow; however, the storm killed large numbers of wildlife and domestic livestock alike. John Winthrop of New London reported that at his farm on Fishers Island, more than 1,100 sheep, along with some cows and horses, were buried beneath the snow, where they froze to death. Two sheep survived twenty-eight days entombed in the snow, supposedly by eating the wool of dozens of other dead sheep buried with them.

The worst snowstorm in Connecticut history was the blizzard that struck between March 11 and 14 of 1888. The primitive weather forecasting and limited long-distance communication of the time meant residents had no warning of the approach of the nor'easter, which dumped anywhere from eighteen to forty-four inches of snow along the shoreline. Howling winds whipped up drifts as high as thirty-eight feet.

The blizzard paralyzed much of the Northeast, including Connecticut's Long Island Sound coastal towns. Snow clogged roads and railroad tracks, bringing traffic to a standstill.

Blizzard of 1888, snow tunnel, Bridgeport. Someone introduced a bit of whimsy to the task of clearing away tons of snow from Bridgeport's streets and sidewalks by carving a tunnel through a mound of snow and making it available "to rent."

Blizzard of 1888, clearing train tracks, South Norwalk. Workers paused from their labors to pose with towering mountains of snow they shoveled by hand from the New York, New Haven & Hartford Railroad's tracks in South Norwalk.

Blizzard of 1888, Cannon Street, Bridgeport. Snow cleaned from roadways and sidewalks in cities accumulated into giant mounds that served as a craggy playscape for children, like these youngsters on Cannon Street in Bridgeport.

People were trapped in their homes, in their places of work, in train stations. Some of those who bravely—or foolishly—ventured out into the brutally cold, often blinding storm paid for their poor judgment with their lives. Two women who left the Bridgeport factory where they worked were found two days later in a snowdrift, frozen to death.

Summer Storms

Hurricanes are much rarer occurrences than snowstorms along the Connecticut coast, but when they hit, they can deliver unimaginable death and destruction in a few short hours.

One of the most powerful hurricanes to strike the Connecticut shore blew in early on Saturday, September 23, 1815. In New London at the height of the storm, "the

Hurricane of 1938: Grove Beach, Clinton. The damage and destruction wrought on Clinton's Grove Beach was repeated in town after town along the Sound.

Hurricane of 1938: Hawk's Nest, Old Lyme. What only a day or so earlier was a waterfront cottage at Hawk's Nest in Old Lyme had been reduced to a pile of splintered lumber and scrap.

Hurricane of 1938; **Tulip** ***on shore, New London.*** The storm tossed the lightship tender *Tulip* up and over the railroad tracks on the New London waterfront.

Hurricane of 1938: train off tracks, Stonington. The raging hurricane pushed both train and tracks right off the railroad causeway into Stonington. There were only two deaths thanks to the quick-thinking engineer, who shifted passengers into the forward cars, which he then separated from the rest of the train before it was forced off the causeway.

lower parts of the town had now become the scenes of devastation and distress," reported the *New London Gazette*. "The stores were falling, the wharves had disappeared, the vessels rushing on shore or crushing each other in the docks, buildings unroofing, the trees falling and the air filled with flying fragments, while men, women and children were seen supplicating help from the windows of their dwellings." More than four dozen buildings along with a number of vessels were seriously damaged or destroyed in the city, but no lives were reported lost.

Stonington was not so fortunate. Every ship in the harbor was run aground. One was crushed to splinters, its crew rescued by local residents. Approximately thirty structures suffered damage or were lost completely.

"But the most heart rending scene, was a dwelling house floating off with its inhabitants" in Stonington, according to the *New London Gazette*. The owner, shipbuilder Benjamin Morell, had left his home to go to the aid of neighbors. While he was away, reported the *Gazette*, "the sea surrounded his dwelling, and before relief could be given, it was swept from its foundations, and its wretched inhabitants, Mrs. Morell, and child, and a Miss Mott of Block-Island, were buried in a watery grave."

Almost to the exact day 123 years later, the Connecticut coast was struck by a storm that was not only its most devastating hurricane ever, but the worst natural disaster in Connecticut history. As with the Blizzard of 1888, weather forecasting in 1938 was still so unsophisticated that a warning couldn't be issued in time for anyone to evacuate before the hurricane hit. As a result, many people were in their beachfront cottages and homes when the storm struck on September 21, 1938, with an eighteen-foot storm surge and winds exceeding 125 miles per hour.

The damage was greatest in communities east of New Haven, which did not have the partial protection of Long Island to the south serving as a buffer to the advancing storm. In town after town, hundreds of shoreline cottages were shoved off their foundations, sliced in half, or completely smashed. In some places one-third of the structures were flattened.

New London suffered the most damage from the Hurricane of '38. Fire erupted in the storm's wake, burning for seven hours and destroying a significant portion of the waterfront area. Losses were estimated at $4 million—more than $100 million in twenty-first-century dollars.

The death toll was tragically high: More than one hundred Connecticut residents died. Unaware of how ferocious the impending storm was, many tried to ride it out in waterfront cottages and were swept to their deaths. Stratford resident Mrs. Leroy Lewis, who had just become the Republican Party nominee for secretary of state, making her the first woman ever nominated for a state office, was killed along with her husband when their summer house on one of the Thimble Islands off Stony Creek was washed away. Thousands of people in Connecticut were injured, and dozens were reported missing.

WATERFORD

21.

*W*aterford. It's a pleasantly prosaic name, supposedly inspired in part by the ability to ford the Jordan Brook, which runs nearly the entire length of the town. But it doesn't hint at the extremes—fierce controversy, backbreaking labor, lavish elegance—that have featured prominently in more than 350 years of history.

Waterford was settled in 1653 as part of New London, to which it belonged for nearly the next 150 years. Before the seventeenth century ended, a fundamental disagreement over matters of faith developed into an ugly, ongoing battle between dissenters and the establishment.

In the 1670s, members of the family of James Rogers, one of the richest men in New London, became affiliated with Baptists in nearby Rhode Island. After a few years James Rogers's son John, who lived in the part of New London that today is Waterford, organized his parents, brothers, and a few other followers into their own religious sect, with unorthodox beliefs. They came to be called Rogerenes, for their leader, John Rogers.

The Rogerenes disagreed with many fundamental tenets of the Congregational Church, which was the established faith of Connecticut. Rogerenes would not attend Sabbath worship services at the Congregational meetinghouse as required by law and refused to pay taxes to support the church because they didn't attend it. They dressed in plain clothes, refused to swear oaths, opposed baptizing infants, and were pacifists.

The Rogerenes might have been allowed to practice their own faith largely unmolested by the government, but they were dedicated to provoking authorities whenever possible. They "courted persecution and gloried in it," in the words of one historian. If they stayed away from Sunday services, they would compound their violation of the law by working at their routine occupations. If they did come to the meetinghouse, they brought along something to work on as a demonstration of their conviction that the Sabbath was no holier a day than any other in the week. They would interrupt the minister in the midst of preaching and challenge him on the points he was making in his sermon.

For their infractions, the Rogerenes were repeatedly punished by the authorities. They were fined, and when they refused to pay, imprisoned. Some were whipped for their offenses. John Rogers endured more than any of the others. In 1706 he claimed that he had "been sentenced to pay hundreds of pounds, laid in iron chains, cruelly scourged, endured long imprisonments, set in the stocks many hours together."

John and his family lived in the area called Mamacoke in northeastern Waterford, not far from the Thames River. From their original affiliation with the Baptists, and their

Fort Trumbull

Warren Gates, the first man to quarry Waterford granite for building, supplied the federal government with the stone to build the current Fort Trumbull in New London. It was constructed between 1839 and 1852 in the Egyptian Revival style. Millstone granite would be used to construct part or all of a string of defensive forts built during the 1840s at harbors from Rhode Island to Alabama.

By 1847 more than two dozen men were laboring in the Millstone Quarry to fill the large federal contract and those from other clients. A small community of workers' homes grew up not far from the quarry, called, appropriately, Graniteville. Warren Gates built himself a home in Graniteville, as did his successor, John Palmer.

A Legacy of Beauty for All to Enjoy

Edward Harkness spent his life giving away much of the vast fortune inherited from his father, who had been a partner in the Standard Oil Company. He was a benefactor of many institutions, including Yale University and Connecticut College in Connecticut, but his most significant philanthropic endeavor was the New York–based Commonwealth Fund, the goal of which is to improve the health care system for all Americans.

In 1907 Harkness and his wife, Mary, completed construction of a house on Goshen Point overlooking Long Island Sound. The forty-two-room mansion, called Eolia after the island on which the Greek god of the winds resided, was built of fireproof concrete—the construction material that would hasten the demise of Waterford's granite quarries. To design the gardens and grounds, the Harknesses retained Beatrix Jones Farrand, one of the first women to become a professional landscape architect.

The Eolia estate was also the site of some of the Harknesses' philanthropic activities. In 1920 Mary Harkness established a summer camp for children from New York City who had contracted polio. The camp operated until it was interrupted by World War II.

Edward Harkness died in 1940, and Eolia and its 325 acres became the property of the state of Connecticut. More than two hundred acres, including the house, were turned into Harkness Memorial State Park. Although decades of neglect allowed Eolia to deteriorate into a near ruin, a multimillion-dollar restoration begun in 1996 returned both the building and its lovely gardens to their appearance in the 1930s.

Shanties at Millstone, July 31, 1885

A woman in the doorway watches a boy who stands triumphantly atop one of the blocks of granite that litter the yard around what a notation on the back of the photograph identifies as "Shanties at Millstone, July 31, 1885." A building boom in the 1870s created a huge demand for granite. Immigrants—first coming from England, Scotland, and Ireland, later from Sweden, Finland, and Italy—filled many of the jobs that opened up at Millstone and other Waterford quarries. At one point Millstone alone employed as many as four hundred workers.

Maypole at Sandy Point, July, 1885

Even as Waterford's quarries attracted laborers, other areas of town drew those with leisure time to spend, like the group of adults and children depicted dancing around a maypole. An inscription on the back identifies the occasion as "Agnes Birthday Fete, July, 1885," and the location as a "Cottage at Sandy Point, Niantic River, Ct." Sandy Point juts into the Niantic River at its northern end.

later involvement with a Quaker preacher, the Rogerenes came to be known, variously and incorrectly, as Rogerene Quakers or Rogerene Baptists. This misunderstanding resulted in the portion of Waterford in which they settled and proliferated being called Quaker Hill.

Unlike some sects that have formed around a powerful leader, the Rogerenes did not fall apart after John Rogers died in 1721. His son and descendants of several of the other original members guided the small group for generations. The Rogerenes remained a facet of southeastern Connecticut's religious culture into the twentieth century.

Waterford was incorporated from New London as a separate town in 1801. Residents soon began to heed, long before it became a bit of pop culture wisdom, the advice that "when life hands you lemons, make lemonade." They turned acres of stony land unfit for farming into quarries that would be one of the town's thriving industries for close to a century.

The earliest English settlers had valued Waterford's stone—specifically granite. In 1651, John Winthrop Jr. gained possession of hundreds of acres on the eastern side of Niantic Bay. Soon granite deposits on the land were being quarried to make millstones—large, round stones used to grind grain. These were used locally and also sold to the West Indies. The area became known as "Millstone."

Millstones were the only significant use to which Waterford granite was put for the next 180 years. In 1788, 138 acres of the Millstone property were acquired by Benajah Gardiner. Beginning in the 1830s, his descendants leased portions of the quarry to a series of men who employed laborers to extract the stone. The heavy blocks had to be moved only a short distance overland to reach water deep enough to accommodate large ships. The granite was loaded onto vessels that transported them to customers along the Atlantic seaboard.

In the decades following the Civil War, most of the granite quarried in Waterford went to pave the streets of major cities, including Boston, New Orleans, Philadelphia, and New York, as well as New Haven and New London. Demand for that purpose increased with the arrival of automobiles, which needed as smooth a surface as possible over which to run.

Around 1890, seven brothers from Scotland named Booth acquired a quarrying lease at Millstone. They hit a roadblock in 1893 when Henry Gardiner, a descendant of Benajah Gardiner, decided to stop leasing the quarrying operation to others and run it himself. Gardiner introduced steam power at Millstone and built a rail spur to the quarry so that the stone could be shipped out both by water or train.

The Booth brothers, meanwhile, wasted no time setting up on their own. They had purchased seventy acres on the opposite side of the Niantic River, close to Jordan Cove. There they opened what became Waterford's second largest quarry.

Smaller granite quarries opened elsewhere in Waterford, including in the Quaker Hill district. Ultimately there were seven in town.

The early years of the twentieth century were the heyday of granite quarrying in Waterford. There followed a slow but steady decline in an industry that had shaped the town's population and economy for generations. The major culprits were concrete, which replaced granite in new buildings, and asphalt and blacktop, which were superior alternatives for paving.

The smaller quarries closed in the 1920s. Millstone, Booth Brothers, and another quarry, Flat Rock, stayed in business, but the hurricane of 1938 severely damaged their facilities. Booth Brothers closed in 1940; Flat Rock in 1941; Millstone in 1963.

The quarries that once employed hundreds of Waterford workers have all but vanished. Where the Flat Rock Quarry was located, the Crystal Mall sits today. The Booth Brothers quarry is overgrown and filled with water. And the Millstone Quarry, the first and the longest lived, is now the site of a nuclear power plant that has generated more and farther-reaching controversy than even the Rogerenes did.

In 1951 three electric utility companies joined forces to purchase 114 acres at the Millstone Quarry, intending to build a coal-burning generating plant. In 1962 the plan was revised to call for an electric generating plant run by nuclear power. More quarry land was purchased, for a total of five hundred acres. The first nuclear reactor began operating in 1970, and by 1986 two more had been constructed.

In the 1990s it was revealed that Nuclear Regulatory Commission safety regulations were not being adequately enforced at the Millstone Power Station, and in 1996 the commission ordered all three reactors to cease operation until the problems were corrected. The original reactor, Millstone I, never went back into service. The other two reactors were up and running again by 2000, but controversy over whether the Millstone reactors pose any danger to public health and the environment continues.

Like the quarries it replaced, the Millstone Power Station has a profound effect on Waterford's economy. Dominion Nuclear, which purchased Millstone in 2000, was the largest employer in town in 2004, and its facilities made up fully a third of the grand list that year.

22

NEW LONDON

The English settlement now known as New London was originally called Pequot, and the river was known as the Mohegan. Residents wanted to name the new town after the great city of London in their native land, but the Connecticut General Assembly would not agree. In 1658, after a decade-long standoff, the assembly gave in and bestowed upon Pequot the new name of New London. The river assumed the name, perhaps inevitably, of the Thames, after the one that flows through the original London. However, it was pronounced, for some unknown reason, as if it rhymed with the word *games,* and not "Tems" like its English counterpart.

Like their namesakes across the Atlantic, New London and the Thames became important centers of seafaring and related economic activities. Shipbuilding began in the 1660s and continued for more than two centuries.

By the middle of the eighteenth century, dozens of New London ships were trading with ports on the North American coast from Newfoundland to Georgia, and, most importantly, with islands in the West Indies. The sea could provide a good living but could also extract a high price from those who sought to do so. Storms could damage ships and spoil cargo, or even send a vessel to the bottom of the sea with its entire crew. Ships were at risk of attack by vessels of whatever nation Great Britain might be at war with at the time. Disease and accidents resulted in many untimely deaths for a large number of young sailors. Capt. Nathaniel Shaw Sr. of New London lost three sons at sea, all in their early twenties.

The outbreak of the American Revolution brought an abrupt halt to New London's maritime trade, for the enemy British ruled the seas. Many Connecticut ship owners turned to another line of work: privateering. Privateers were privately owned vessels that a government—in this instance, the State of Connecticut—authorized in time of war to hunt down and capture both military and civilian ships owned by the enemy.

Joshua Hempsted House, ca. 1950s

New London was a fledgling settlement barely thirty years old when the Joshua Hempsted House was built in 1678. That same year Joshua Hempsted was born in what would be his home until his death in 1758. For nearly fifty years Hempsted kept a diary that offers a rare glimpse into life within the walls of this house and in the broader community. The daily routine in colonial Connecticut as revealed by Hempsted's diary entries included mundane chores and personal tragedy.

The Joshua Hempsted House was one of the few buildings to escape destruction in the fire that ravaged most of New London during the 1781 British raid. It is one of the oldest and best-documented buildings in New England

Privateers brought vessels they seized into port, where ship and cargo were sold. The proceeds were distributed among the owners, investors, and crew. Manned by sailors motivated by the possibility of great financial gain, privateers inflicted far more damage on the enemy British during the Revolution than the small official navy did. The prizes they captured often contained goods desperately needed by the patriot forces, including weapons and clothing.

New London was home to more privateers—fifty-nine—than any other Connecticut port. They captured 157 prizes. This record earned it a reputation that attracted the unwelcome attention of the British, who made it the target of a major raid late in the war.

Shaw Mansion (Washington's Headquarters), ca. 1901–1907

The nerve center of Connecticut's naval participation in the American Revolution was the home of Nathaniel Shaw Jr., built in 1758. Shaw was an enormously wealthy merchant who traded with the West Indies and Europe up until the outbreak of the American Revolution in 1775. The Connecticut government soon put Shaw in charge of its tiny fleet of barely more than a dozen ships and, much more important to the war effort, authorized him to commission privateers, dozens of which sailed from New London alone. The Shaw mansion was set on fire by British raiders in 1781. Luckily, the flames were extinguished before major damage occurred.

On September 6, 1781, two dozen British vessels landed approximately 1,700 soldiers at the mouth of the Thames River. The invaders embarked on a two-pronged attack—half marching up the eastern bank to Fort Griswold, the other half up the western bank to New London.

Commanding the raid was Benedict Arnold, the Norwich native who the previous year had turned traitor and gone over to the British, receiving a general's commission in the enemy's army. The purpose of the mission was to destroy privateers and their prizes anchored in the Thames, along with any supplies stored in the riverfront warehouses. But it resulted in wholesale death and destruction.

On the Groton side, the defenders of Fort Griswold put up a valiant fight against overwhelming numbers of the enemy. When the British finally captured the fort, they mercilessly slaughtered more than eighty of its garrison and grievously wounded dozens more.

In New London, the British went about setting fire to vessels and supplies. Although Arnold claimed destruction of private homes was not part of the enemy's plan, the blaze

AMERICAN WHALER.

American Whaler, ca. 1850–1851

More than 250 ships like the vessel depicted in this lithograph sailed from New London to hunt whales. Each of the one thousand voyages made from New London was a high-stakes gamble: The owner, captain, or investor in a whaler could grow rich from the profits of a whaling voyage, which might last for years and take a ship to the farthest reaches of the globe, or the vessel might simply disappear, never to be heard from again, sunk by a storm or by damage inflicted by its gigantic quarry.

Whale Oil Row, ca. 1880–1889

The wealth that could be realized from whaling is represented by the four houses on Huntington Street known as "Whale Oil Row." Residents of the quartet of dwellings, built between 1833 and 1845 in the popular Greek Revival style, included Thomas Williams, owner of ten whalers, and Enoch Stoddard, owner of eleven.

New London, 1876

Whaling was winding down as New London's biggest source of revenue by the time this 1876 bird's-eye view was published, but industry had stepped in to take up at least part of the slack. The Brown Cotton Gin Manufactory, established in 1858, turned out the product for which it was named for sixty years. The even older Albertson & Douglass Machine Company manufactured a line of goods that included cotton gins, steam engines, and iron railings. New London firms also fabricated horse nails, woolen fabric, and hardware.

New London was also developing as a summer resort. The Pequot House, opened in 1853, was popular with wealthy vacationers from New York and Washington, D.C. When the crush of visitors proved more than the hotel could accommodate, cottages or "villas" were built to handle the overflow. The Pequot House was destroyed by fire in 1908.

State Street, 1875

A photograph taken in 1875 reveals that State Street looking toward New London Harbor wasn't quite the tidy byway depicted in the 1876 bird's-eye-view. Horse-drawn wagons and carriages line the side of the street, signs protrude out over it, and the dirt road is rutted.

quickly spread to these and other structures. Most of the city was soon in flames, with more than 140 buildings and many ships reduced to ashes, and it took a long time for New London to recover from the devastation.

Looking back in time, to New London's establishment in the mid-1600s, it had included the modern towns of Ledyard, Groton, Montville, and Waterford, as well as parts of Salem and East Lyme. It was whittled down over the course of a century, beginning with the incorporation of Groton (which then also included Ledyard) as a town in 1705. Montville and part of Salem separated from New London in 1786, and finally Waterford and part of East Lyme in 1801, leaving New London as Connecticut's littlest town from a geographic standpoint.

Reduced in size and devastated by the American Revolution, New London's commercial rebirth began in 1819, with a fresh focus on an activity that had been pursued only marginally for a century: whaling. Whale oil was in heavy demand for candles and lamps, among other uses, and within thirty years New London had become one of the nation's busiest whaling ports, surpassed only by New Bedford, Massachusetts, and sometimes the island of Nantucket.

Whaling became the foundation of New London's revived economy. Many merchants who owned whaling ships reaped large fortunes. Most residents who did not own or actually sail on the whalers made their living at some occupation connected to the enterprise, including shipbuilding, crafting of equipment, or preparing supplies for the voyages, which could last a year or two or even longer.

Men's outing, New London or vicinity, ca. 1897–1898

A group of men out for a summer's day of baseball and beer at a site somewhere in or near New London around 1897–1898 take a break to pose for a photograph. Whether the men worked for Charles P. Swan's New London moving company, to which the vehicle behind them belonged, or hired one of Swan's horse-drawn moving vehicles for the day, is unknown.

New London's whaling heyday lasted for barely half a century. By the beginning of the Civil War in 1861, the industry was experiencing a decline caused by several factors, among which the replacement of whale oil by kerosene was the most important. By the end of the war, New London had fewer than a third as many whalers as it had in 1849. New London whalers would be completely gone by the end of the nineteenth century.

However, another industry had begun to emerge in New London even before the Civil War: tourism. New London became a popular summer resort for urbanites, particularly New Yorkers, and in the later decades of the nineteenth century, cottages sprang up to accommodate families who wished to stay for an entire summer. One of these vacation homes provided inspiration for one of America's greatest playwrights: Eugene O'Neill.

O'Neill was born in 1888 into an acting family that spent most of its time on the road, traveling from theater to theater. As a result, the only thing approaching a permanent, stable home that O'Neill knew for nearly the first thirty years of his life was the family's summer house on the Thames River in New London. It was called Monte Cristo cottage after O'Neill's father's most renowned acting role, the Count of Monte Cristo.

The Monte Cristo cottage was the setting for two of O'Neill's greatest plays, *Ah! Wilderness* and the brutally autobiographical *Long Day's Journey Into Night*. O'Neill received four Pulitzer prizes for his work and was the first American playwright to be awarded the Nobel Prize for literature.

The twentieth century saw New London act aggressively to introduce higher education into the fabric of the city's life. In 1909, just as record numbers of women were enrolling in college, Wesleyan University in Middletown, Connecticut, decided to cease accepting women. A plan to establish a women's college in Connecticut was formed. New London residents raised $135,000—the equivalent of more than $3 million in modern dollars—in ten days to secure the honor of being home to the new school, Connecticut College for Women, which opened in 1911. Today the school, called Connecticut College (since it began accepting men), has a student body of 1,900.

New London's civic generosity also lured the U.S. Coast Guard to establish its permanent home in the city, thereby continuing the community's historic connection with the sea. The Coast Guard's training facility had been located in New London at Fort Trumbull since 1910, and in 1932 New London gave the land on which the current academy is located. Approximately one thousand students are enrolled in the Coast Guard Academy today.

23.

GROTON

For any town geography is destiny, but that seems to have been particularly true for Groton. Flanked on the west by the Thames River with its excellent harbor, on the east by the Mystic River, and with Long Island Sound as its southern boundary, it was almost inevitable that Groton's development would be dominated by building, outfitting, and sailing vessels. Whether powered by wind, steam, or nuclear fission, Groton-made ships have for more than three centuries navigated the globe on voyages of commerce, fishing, recreation, and, above all, national defense.

The Pequot tribe of Native Americans occupied what today is Groton for at least half a century before the first Europeans arrived, and then tragedy befell Groton's original inhabitants during the Pequot War of 1636–1637. English settlers from Massachusetts and Connecticut, allied with Mohegan and Narragansett Indians, killed or sent into slavery the vast majority of Pequots. On a single night in May of 1637, more than seven hundred Pequots, primarily women and children, were slain in a gruesome ambush on their village in the Mystic section of Groton.

English settlers began moving to the eastern bank of the Thames River, then part of New London, in the 1650s. In 1705 the land between the Thames and Mystic Rivers became a separate town. It was called Groton, the name originally given to a land grant in what today is Bluff Point State Park by John Winthrop Jr., in honor of his birthplace in England.

Shipbuilding was under way in Groton by the 1680s, and within half a century it had developed into an industry so advanced in scope and skill that the largest commercial sailing vessel built in North America prior to the American Revolution was constructed here. The shipbuilding industry stimulated the growth of a community of craftsmen who produced essential equipment, including blacksmiths, coopers, sailmakers, and rope makers. When completed, a vessel needed a crew, and many a Groton man went to sea.

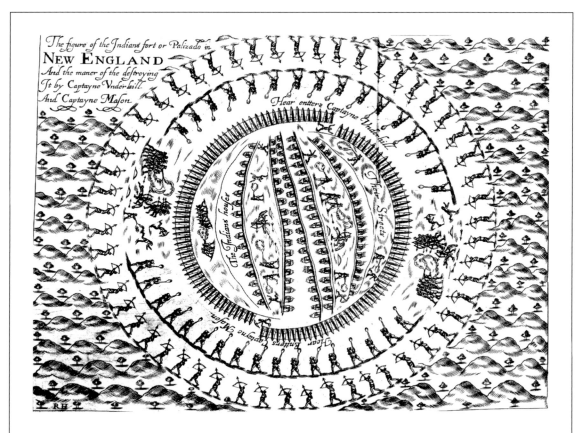

The figure of the Indian fort or Palizado in New England And the maner of the destroying it by Captayne Underhill and Captayne Mason, 1637

Capt. John Underhill included this meticulously detailed woodcut of the destruction of a Pequot village by troops commanded by him and Capt. John Mason in his 1638 book Newes from America, *published in London. War between the English settlers of Massachusetts and Connecticut and the Pequots erupted in 1636, and on May 26, 1637, Underhill and Mason led a force of colonists and Mohegan and Narragansett Indian allies in a surprise nighttime attack on the Pequot fort in the Mystic section of Groton.*

The Pequot fort, which covered about an acre and was protected by a stockade of tree trunks, is shown in the center, surrounded by English colonists with muskets, backed up by Native Americans armed with bows and arrows. The English invaded the fort, which contained as many as seven hundred Pequots, mostly women and children.

The Pequots fought back so fiercely that Underhill and Mason decided to set fire to the fort. Some Pequots refused to leave and died in the flames, still fighting. Those who tried to flee were cut down by colonists with musket and sword or by Native Americans with bow and arrow. Underhill wrote that immediately following the slaughter, "so many soules lie gasping on the ground so thicke in some places, that you could hardly passe along." Only a handful of Pequots escaped alive.

The outbreak of the American Revolution in 1775 opened an era of unprecedented opportunity—and risk—in Groton's history and also led to its greatest tragedy. The rebellious colonies, at war with the world's greatest sea power, had no official navy to speak of. Connecticut began granting privately owned ships official permission to attack and seize any vessel, military or private, belonging to the enemy British—a practice called privateering.

This "legalized piracy," as some have called it, was routinely practiced by European nations during war. The odds of success were small, but captain and crew were highly motivated because they received a portion of the proceeds from the sale of any captured vessel and its cargo brought into port. Dozens of civilian ships armed themselves and sailed forth

Groton Monument and Fort Griswold, ca. 1835

In 1830 the State of Connecticut erected a 127-foot-tall granite obelisk near Fort Griswold to honor the men who had fought and died defending that bastion against a British invasion in 1781. The state authorized a lottery to raise funds for the monument, shown in this sketch from around 1835. In 1881 the height of the monument was increased to 134 feet. The obelisk, along with the remains of the Revolutionary War fortifications, including stone walls, trenches, and earthworks, today is part of the Fort Griswold Battlefield State Park.

PLANT RESIDENCE, GROTON, CONN.

M. F. Plant's Residence, ca. 1910

In 1903, Morton Plant spent $3 million (the equivalent of at least $60 million in the twenty-first century) of the fortune he inherited to build this spectacular granite Tudor mansion on Avery Point, a scenic spur of land extending into Long Island Sound. Plant's wife, who studied architecture in Paris, worked with English architect Robert W. Gibson to design the thirty-one-room "Branford House," named for the Connecticut town of Morton Plant's birth.

Branford House's eclectic interior included rooms designed in styles from Romantic to Gothic. Expert artisans by the hundreds were brought from Europe to craft the costly wood, stone, and metal decorative features.

Morton Plant himself developed the grounds of Branford House, where he typically spent just a month or two every summer, into a horticulturist's delight. The extensive gardens included whatever pleased Plant's fancy, such as tropical plants that had to be dug up to spend the winter in a heated conservatory until spring brought weather warm enough to replant them outside. Italian stoneworkers furnished the garden with marble statues, pools, and fountains. Plant also developed a three-hundred-acre farm on which he raised fruits, vegetables, cattle, and poultry.

When Plant died in 1918, Branford House was inherited by his son. Astonishingly, it was auctioned off in 1939 for a pittance of what it cost to build. Acquired by the State of Connecticut, it was conveyed in 1941 to the U.S. Coast Guard. During World War II, Morton Plant's cherished gardens, including the marble statuary, were razed—literally pushed over the nearby cliff—and barracks built in their place.

In 1967 Branford House became the Avery Point Branch of the University of Connecticut. The building has since been refurbished.

Town Hall, Groton, Conn.   Presentation of Loving Cup, in behalf of Groton to Morton F. Plant, donor of building, at Dedication, Sept. 17th 1908.

30200

Published by J. Solomon, New London, Conn.

Town Hall dedication, 1908

Millionaire Morton Plant, who summered at his Avery Point mansion Branford House, was a generous philanthropist whose gifts included $25,000 to Groton to build a town hall. A crowd assembled for the dedication on September 17, 1908, at which the town presented Plant with a loving cup as a token of its appreciation.

from Groton and from New London across the Thames. Connecticut privateers and their counterparts from other states greatly hampered the British at sea, while the cargoes they captured were a source of supplies desperately needed by the patriot forces.

Late in July of 1781, the most valuable ship ever captured by a Connecticut privateer was brought into New London Harbor. Less than a week later, the British moved to clean out what a Tory newspaper called "the most detestable nest of pirates on the continent." On September 6, 1781, 1,700 British, Loyalist, and Hessian troops came ashore at the mouth of the Thames. Commanding the expedition was Benedict Arnold, a native of nearby Norwich who had served gloriously in the patriot army, then stunned everyone by deserting, turning traitor, and becoming a British general.

Gold Star Bridge under construction, ca. 1940

The rapid rise of the automobile resulted in the conversion in 1919 of a railroad bridge (seen in the background) into the first highway bridge to span the Thames River. The Gold Star Bridge, under construction in the foreground, began as a Works Progress Administration project during the Great Depression. The United States' entry into World War II made access to the shipyards and naval installations in Groton and New London of critical importance, and completion of the Gold Star Bridge a priority. It was finished in 1943. The bridge was renovated and widened in the 1970s. Today it is part of Interstate 95.

The invading forces split into two and began marching up both banks of the Thames, intending to set fire to the offending privateers and any captured cargo. Before the sun set, most of New London had gone up in flames.

On the Groton side, 158 men and boys, most hastily summoned volunteers, bravely defended Fort Griswold against repeated assaults by an enemy who outnumbered them five to one. When Fort Griswold's commander, Col. William Ledyard, rejected a demand to surrender the post, the British warned they would henceforth show no mercy to any patriot soldier.

Inevitably the British overwhelmed Fort Griswold's valiant defenders. Colonel Ledyard stepped forward to surrender his command to a British officer, handing over his

First Lady Jacqueline Kennedy christening the USS Lafayette, May 8, 1962

On May 8, 1962, First Lady Jacqueline Kennedy broke the traditional bottle of champagne to christen the nuclear-powered submarine USS Lafayette at the Electric Boat Division of General Dynamics in Groton. The official history of the submarine notes that for the occasion the always-stylish Mrs. Kennedy wore a "chartreuse Oleg Cassini coat and matching Breton hat."

sword in a gesture of submission. Ledyard was killed on the spot, skewered by a blade wielded by an enemy hand, although reports that he was killed with his own sword appear not to be true.

The victorious enemy proceeded to mercilessly butcher the American garrison. More than eighty patriots were killed, many mangled almost beyond recognition, and dozens more grievously wounded in what quickly became infamous as the Massacre at Fort Griswold. In 1836 when the northern portion of Groton became a separate town, it took the name of Ledyard in honor of the colonel.

With the return of peace in the 1780s, shipbuilding once again flourished in Groton. As the nineteenth century advanced, the number and type of ships produced in Groton changed and grew in response to increasing demand and innovations. Groton built sleek clipper ships designed to make fast voyages to the other side of the continent and splendid yachts for the well-to-do. Steam power was the great technological breakthrough of the nineteenth century, and Groton shipyards included many among their output, including two "ironclad" vessels built for the Union Army during the Civil War.

In addition to making the ships, Groton men continued to man them. Whalers went forth in such numbers that the Thames River became nearly as important a center of whaling as the more famous New Bedford, Massachusetts

For Groton the twentieth century brought the submarine—and developments in seafaring and national defense that would have been unimaginable to previous generations. The first submarine built in Groton was constructed in 1924—for the government of Peru—by the Electric Boat Company, established in 1899. The first U.S. Navy submarine built at Groton was completed by Electric Boat in 1934.

Simultaneously, what would become the nation's submarine headquarters was being established in Groton. In 1872 the federal government made 112 acres on the Thames River into an official navy yard. The first submarines showed up in the second decade of the twentieth century, and in 1917 the Groton facility became the home and training ground of the U.S. Navy's submarine force, a role it continues to fill today.

The United States' entry into World War II in 1941 created a critical need for submarines, and Electric Boat proved equal to the massive task. Over the course of four years, Electric Boat produced a total of seventy-four submarines—one approximately every two weeks. The achievements of Electric Boat and the submarine base during World War II earned Groton the nickname of "Submarine Capital of the World." That claim to fame was reaffirmed in 1951 when the U.S. Navy awarded Electric Boat the contract to build the world's first nuclear-powered submarine, the *Nautilus.*

Christened in 1954, the *Nautilus* was in service for more than a quarter of a century. It was the first of dozens of nuclear submarines manufactured in Groton by Electric Boat. Since 1982 the *Nautilus* has been permanently stationed in Groton, and it is a National Historic Landmark.

The destiny shaped by Groton's geography has included more than shipbuilding and seafaring. The town's picturesque location on Long Island Sound made it a popular vacation area, particularly in the early twentieth century. Many private mansions, cottages, and large hotels went up along the coast, and some survive as reminders of Groton's heyday as a getaway.

24.

STONINGTON

Stonington's very name—selected "probably because of the character of the soil," according to historian Henry Robinson Palmer—was an early hint that residents shouldn't expect to live by farming alone. But Stonington's rocky land occupies a great location, right where Long Island Sound meets the Atlantic Ocean. Its people embraced the advantages of being so near the sea—and contended with the disasters that were part of the package.

Settlement of Stonington began in the 1650s. Connecticut, Massachusetts, and Rhode Island squabbled for more than a decade over which had jurisdiction over the town, and the dispute was resolved in 1662 by the royal charter granted to Connecticut, which decreed the Pawcatuck River to be Connecticut's southeastern boundary.

For 150 years following English settlement, Stonington citizens earned much of their livelihood from the sea, fishing for cod and mackerel, trading with towns along the Atlantic coast and as far away as the West Indies. Settlement of Long Point, today's Stonington Borough, didn't commence until after 1750. This area, jutting into the sea, would bear the brunt of hostile assaults, the first during the American Revolution.

In August of 1775, thousands of British troops had been penned up in Boston for four months by patriot forces that had rallied to support Massachusetts minutemen after the outbreak of the war for American independence. The besieged British resorted to sending out ships to scour coastal towns for cattle to feed their soldiers.

When residents of Block Island learned British foragers were approaching, they sent their cattle to Stonington, about seventeen miles away, for safekeeping. The British found out about the evacuation and sailed for Stonington. After rejecting British demands to turn over the cattle, Stonington residents mounted a spirited armed resistance against an enemy landing party that tried to come ashore. Angered by this opposition, the captain

Battle of Stonington, ca. 1818–1825

Massive British vessels menace Long Point in this depiction of the War of 1812 Battle of Stonington on an earthenware pitcher manufactured between 1818 and 1825. Although outnumbered and outgunned, Stonington residents valiantly repelled the enemy in an engagement reminiscent of that between David and Goliath.

The battle commenced on August 9, 1814, when Capt. Thomas Hardy, in command of a British squadron of ships, appeared off Stonington and informed residents that they had one hour to evacuate before he would start bombarding the town. Local officials protested this harsh ultimatum, but in vain. The British vessels, with a combined total of 160 cannon, began shelling Stonington at eight o'clock that evening. The Americans returned fire with the two or three small cannons at their disposal. When several boatloads of British tried to come ashore, they were repulsed.

The British resumed the bombardment the next morning. Again they sent boats filled with men to attempt a landing, and again they were forced to retreat, by an American force that had been strengthened by the arrival of militia responding to an urgent summons for help. The British ships sailed out of range of the patriot cannon and began a bombardment of Stonington that lasted into August 12. Enemy missiles started fires in several buildings they struck, but townspeople managed to put them all out. By the time the British finally broke off the attack on August 12, they had fired several tons of metal at Stonington and suffered more than seventy casualties, including twenty-one dead and fifty wounded. Only one Stonington defender was injured, and the town remained securely in patriot hands.

Philip Freneau, considered by many to be the first significant American poet, wrote "The Battle of Stonington on the Seaboard of Connecticut." This fifteen-stanza work saluted the stalwart defenders and mocked the futile British assault, concluding with:

> *But some assert, on certain grounds,*
> *(Besides the damage and the wounds),*
> *It cost the king ten thousand pounds*
> *To have a dash at Stonington.*

The Morgan at Mystic (No. 2), 1943

During the first six decades of the nineteenth century, a total of more than sixty ships sailed from Stonington in pursuit of whales. Many of the whalers had been built in shipyards on the Mystic River; most were owned by local entrepreneurs. Voyages to hunt whales could last as long as three or four years and involve circling the globe.

The Charles W. Morgan, *the last surviving American wooden whaling vessel, is docked permanently at Mystic Seaport in Stonington. Although the* Morgan *was built in New Bedford in 1841 and did not sail from any Connecticut ports, it nonetheless accurately represents the whalers that ventured out from Stonington.*

Whalers would take on additional men at many of the ports at which they stopped. The result was that the crews of Stonington whalers included sailors from Hawaii, the Philippines, Scotland, the Azores, India, England, the Cape Verde Islands, the West Indies, Portugal, Chile, Denmark, and Norway.

of the British ship proceeded to pound Stonington with cannon fire, fortunately inflicting little damage. The British at last sailed away empty-handed. But they would be back, nearly forty years later—with a vengeance.

Between the end of the American Revolution and the end of the War of 1812, Stonington developed into a port from which vessels set out on round-the-world voyages to hunt seals, whose skins and pelts were in demand primarily for making garments. Ultimately a total of seventeen Stonington ships would engage in the hunt, bringing in as many as one hundred thousand seal skins in a single year. During this period Stonington also had its geographic size reduced by half. In 1807 the town of North Stonington was incorporated.

Stonington had become "conspicuous as a nursery of seamen, distinguished for their enterprise, perseverance and courage," an observer wrote in 1819. Those qualities led one Stonington sea captain to venture more than five hundred miles south of the southern tip of South America, where he encountered something totally unexpected: a new continent. Capt. Nathaniel Palmer, just twenty-one but already in command of the forty-seven-foot-long sloop *Hero,* was searching for seals when on November 17, 1820, he encountered uncharted terra firma that proved to be the first sighting of Antarctica. The area he discovered is called Palmer Land.

Stonington ships were soon also hunting whales for their oil, used to make candles or burned in lamps to light homes and businesses. Whaling became a major industry in

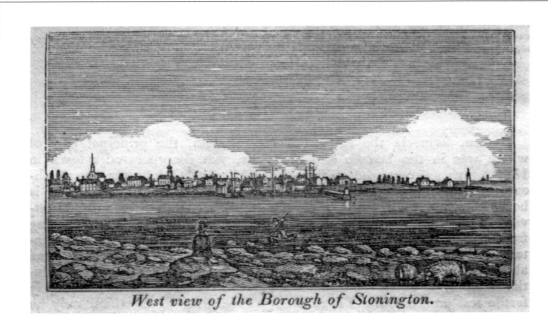

West view of the Borough of Stonington.

West view of the Borough of Stonington, ca. 1835

By 1835 Long Point was Stonington's population center, with about 150 houses and stores and approximately a thousand inhabitants. The community's exposed location, on a peninsula temptingly close to the open ocean, had made it the prime target for the British naval attacks during the American Revolution and the War of 1812.

VIEW OF
STONINGTON, CONN.
G. H. BAILEY & CO., PUBLISHERS, BOSTON.
1879.

View of Stonington, 1879

The railroad-steamship connection inaugurated in 1837 proved so successful that by 1879 a complex of more than half a dozen buildings, including a roundhouse, along with a switching yard and docks, all seen in the left foreground of this bird's-eye view, had been constructed to handle the transfer of passengers and freight. A couple of blocks from the railroad facilities, almost directly above them in this view, stood the Wadawanuck House. This large and lavish hotel, built by railroad officials in 1837 in anticipation of the connection, had sufficient rooms to accommodate more than a thousand guests.

Passengers made the trip between New York and Stonington on massive steamboats like the Stonington, *shown at the dock. On a densely foggy night in 1880, the year after this view was published, the* Stonington *accidentally ran into its sister ship, the* Narragansett, *on Long Island Sound. The* Narragansett *caught fire and went down, and at least several dozen people aboard, perhaps as many as one hundred, were killed. The* Stonington *sustained serious damage but was able to make it back to her namesake port.*

On the very tip of Long Point, to the far right in the view, stands the Stonington Lighthouse, identifiable by the flagpole in front of it. Today the lighthouse is the Stonington Historical Society's headquarters and a museum.

"Church. (Colored.)" Third Baptist Church, ca. 1900

Stonington was one of the few Connecticut towns, along with Hartford, Middletown, New Haven, Bridgeport, and Norwich, in which an African-American church was established prior to the Civil War. The Third Baptist Church, an offshoot of the First Baptist Church, was founded in 1846 with eight members.

From the very beginning the congregation had what every religious body wishes for: its own house of worship. That building, shown in a detail from a bird's-eye view from around 1900, had been a private academy before it was purchased and moved to a lot bought for the purpose.

Church membership reached its height of seventy-three in 1876, and attendance at worship services numbered around 125. From that zenith the church's membership declined, until by 1924 only three members remained. The Third Baptist Church closed its doors, and the church building was sold two years later. It burned down in 1966.

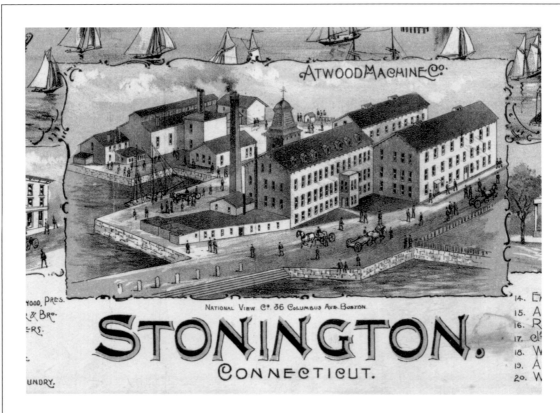

Atwood Machine Company, ca. 1900

John F. Trumbull erected the original granite portion of this factory in 1851. It housed a succession of manufacturing enterprises, including the Joslyn Fire Arms Company, which turned out 16,500 rifles for the Union army cavalry during the Civil War.

In 1876 the facility, shown in a vignette from a bird's-eye view from around 1900, was taken over by the Atwood Machine Company, which manufactured equipment to make silk thread that was sold around the world. The firm flourished for half a century but ultimately fell victim to new technology and products, including the synthetics rayon and nylon, that were introduced in the 1900s. It went out of business at the end of World War II.

Several different companies at various times occupied the building in the succeeding decades. The facility, a fixture of Stonington Borough for more than 150 years, had been vacant for about twenty years when it was destroyed by fire on July 3, 2003.

Stonington, spurring development of the area on the eastern bank of the Mystic River, which is the town's border with Groton. Ultimately a total of more than sixty whalers would sail from Stonington, many built in shipyards that sprang up on both the Stonington and Groton banks of the Mystic River.

Sealing, whaling, and shipbuilding—the mainstays of Stonington's economy for generations—fell on hard times following the Civil War. Hunting sharply reduced the number of seals, and whaling was rendered unprofitable when kerosene replaced whale oil. Mystic shipyards lacked the capabilities to build the new vessels, made of metal and operated by steam, that were superseding wooden, wind-powered ships.

But new businesses gradually filled the void left by the decline in maritime occupations. In 1837 the first rail line in Connecticut was completed in Stonington. The tracks originated in Providence and terminated at the Stonington waterfront, where piers had been built to accommodate steamboats arriving from New York City. This linking of two of the era's latest innovations in transportation would affect Stonington's future for generations.

Prior to the Stonington connection, there were two options for moving people and freight between New York and Providence: overland on horseback or in a stagecoach, or by water, which involved sailing around potentially perilous Point Judith on the Rhode Island coast. Now travelers and cargo could take a steamboat from New York to Stonington, where they transferred to a train that transported them the rest of the way to Providence, or on to Boston if they chose. The combination steamboat/railroad line proved immensely popular and constituted a boom to Stonington's economy. It operated for more than sixty years.

Several Stonington entrepreneurs had the vision to establish factories that provided jobs for those left without work by the decline of the maritime industry. Although John F. Trumbull owned eleven ships, in 1851 he hedged his bets by building a factory in Stonington Borough that would house a series of diverse manufacturing activities for more than a century. In 1894 in Mystic, local leaders raised funds to set up the Rossie Velvet Mill, a branch of a German company, which would operate for decades.

From the beginning of the nineteenth century, sailors who hailed from Chile to Norway, from the West Indies to India, many of them black or of mixed race, had given life in Stonington a multicultural flavor. The town's population became even more diverse with the arrival in the late 1800s and early 1900s of immigrants who were not just in port for a short period but who came to take jobs in factories, in quarries, and on farms. Stonington's population in 1913 was approximately 9,419, and of that number more than 1,100 were of Irish birth or ancestry, 613 of German, 425 Portuguese, and 320 Italian. There were smaller numbers of French Canadians, Austrians, Poles, and Russians as well.

Although World War II brought a population boom as people came to town to work in local industries and also in nearby communities, Stonington's own manufacturing economy suffered setbacks. Two of the major factories closed before the war's end. But Stonington turned once again to the sea, which has provided both traditional and innovative jobs. The only remaining commercial fishing fleet in Connecticut, manned by descendants of Portuguese sailors who originally came to town as crewmen on whaling ships, sails out of Stonington. The town's maritime heritage also provided the raw material for development of a new industry: tourism.

In 1929 Mystic Seaport Museum was established, and it has become one of the state's major tourist attractions, drawing more than three hundred thousand visitors annually. In 1973 what is today the Mystic Aquarium and Institute for Exploration was founded, its location selected because of the region's centuries-old connection to the sea. The stone lighthouse built at Stonington Point in 1840 to guide mariners safely into port now guides tourists on an exploration of the town's heritage.

Looking Back

COASTAL FISHING AND SHELLFISHING

Native Americans enjoyed the fish and shellfish that abounded in Long Island Sound and the rivers that flow into it long before the first Europeans arrived in Connecticut. For the first two centuries after English settlement, residents of coastal towns feasted on the many different varieties of fish that thronged the nearby waters. Many people made a good living catching fish or harvesting oysters for export as far away as Europe or the western coast of North America.

oyster Huts on milford Pt

p. 238

Oyster Huts on Milford Pt., ca. 1835. More than a dozen oyster huts like these stood on Milford Point in the mid-1830s, and during the winter as many as sixty people occupied the small buildings while they harvested oysters. In the foreground are what appear to be piles of oyster shells discarded after their tasty contents were removed.

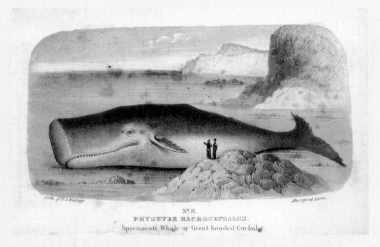

No. 8.
PHYSETER MACROCEPHALUS.
Spermaceti Whale or Great headed Cachalot.

No. 8 Physeter Macrocephalus, Spermaceti Whale or Great headed Cachalot, 1851–1853. Whales, of course, are mammals, not fish, but for much of the nineteenth century they were one of the most valuable creatures pulled from the sea by ships that sailed forth from many Connecticut coastal towns, including New London and Stonington. Despite apparently having been beached and destined for dissection, this sperm whale, hunted for its oil, which was used for lighting and to make candles, has a curiously contented expression.

Eastern Fish Company, New Haven, ca. 1880s. The variety of fish and shellfish available along the coast in the late nineteenth century is evident in the offerings of New Haven's Eastern Fish Company in the 1880s. Oysters, mackerel, shad, salmon, halibut, flounder, trout, pickerel—and fresh boiled lobster for ten cents a pound!

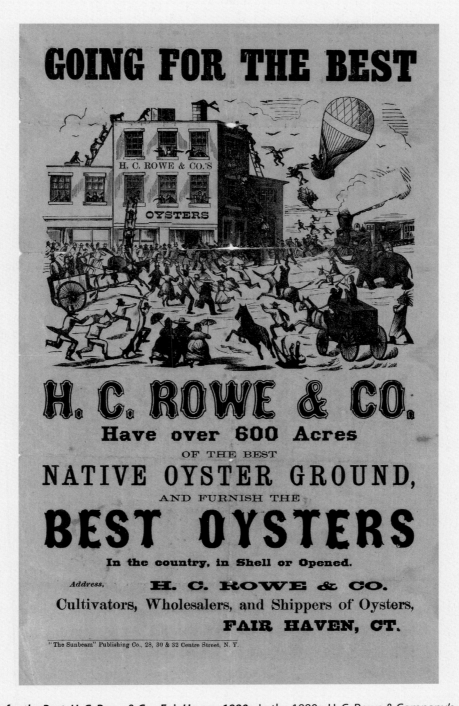

Going for the Best. H. C. Rowe & Co., Fair Haven, 1880s. In the 1880s, H. C. Rowe & Company's whimsically fantastical broadside offered the public nothing less than "the best oysters in the country," harvested from its six hundred acres of oyster grounds off the Fair Haven section of New Haven.

FRESH DAILY ARRIVAL OF SEA FOOD FOR PEASE HOUSE, SAYBROOK POINT, CONN.

Fresh early arrival of seafood for Pease House, Saybrook Point, ca. 1930s. Restaurants and hotels in coastal towns could feed their customers the freshest fruits of the sea thanks to deliveries like this one being made to the Pease House at Saybrook Point.

It's almost impossible to conceive of how many fish and shellfish at one time populated Connecticut's rivers and the Sound. Shad were once so plentiful that they were considered as fit food only for the poorest people; to accuse someone of eating shad was meant as an insult. Salmon were abundant in several of the rivers, and clams and oysters were easy to harvest and inexpensive.

That bounty eventually declined, caused by several factors. Pollution of the waterways, parasites, overfishing, and construction of dams that blocked the way to spawning grounds upriver played roles in the decrease and even near disappearance of many fish and shellfish. Efforts to clean up the rivers and the Sound, and to reintroduce certain species, like salmon in the Connecticut River, have been important steps toward preserving or restoring some of the creatures that once flourished in Connecticut waters.

For more than thirty years, the Norwalk Seaport Association has sponsored an annual oyster festival to celebrate the mollusk's continuing role in its heritage. Since 1973 the town of Clinton has been the site of an annual Bluefish Festival—bluefish being especially coveted by sport fishermen for the fierce fight they put up when on the line.

BIBLIOGRAPHY

Ancestry.com

Barber, John Warner. *Connecticut Historical Collections.* 2nd ed. New Haven: Durrie & Peck and J. W. Barber, 1836.

Bickford, Christopher B., and J. Bard McNulty, eds. *John Warner Barber's Views of Connecticut Towns, 1834–36.* Hartford: The Acorn Club and The Connecticut Historical Society, 1990.

Connecticut Economic Resource Center. www.cerc.com

Crofut, Florence S. Marcy. *Guide to the History and the Historic Sites of Connecticut.* 2 vols. New Haven: Yale University Press, under the Auspices of the Tercentenary Commission of the State of Connecticut for the Connecticut Daughters of the American Revolution, 1937.

East, Robert Abraham. *Connecticut's Loyalists.* Chester, CT: Pequot Press, 1974.

History of Middlesex County, Connecticut, With Biographical Sketches of Its Prominent Men. New York: J. B. Beers & Co., 1884.

McDevitt, Robert. *Connecticut Attacked: A British Viewpoint, Tryon's Raid on Danbury.* Chester, CT: Pequot Press for the American Revolution Bicentennial Commission of Connecticut, 1974.

Miller, James W., and Priscilla W. Dundon, eds. *As We Were on the Valley Shore: An Informal Pictorial History of Sixteen Connecticut Towns.* N.p.: Shore Line Times Co., 1976.

Schoelwer, Susan P., ed. *Lions & Eagles & Bulls: Early American Tavern & Inn Signs from The Connecticut Historical Society.* Hartford: The Connecticut Historical Society in association with Princeton University Press, 2000.

Tucker, Louis Leonard. *Connecticut's Seminary of Sedition: Yale College.* Chester, CT: Pequot Press for the American Revolution Bicentennial Commission of Connecticut, 1974.

Tyler, John W. *Connecticut Loyalists: An Analysis of Loyalist Land Confiscation in Greenwich, Stamford, and Norwalk.* New Orleans: Polyanthos Press, 1977.

Branford

Bouley, Jane, and Pam Knapp. "A Celebration of Ella Wheeler Wilcox, Poet, Journalist, and Progressive Thinker." Branford Historical Society. www.branfordhistory.org/ellawheelerwilcox.html

Branford, Connecticut. www.branford-ct.gov/History

"Branford, Connecticut." Wikipedia. http://en.wikipedia.org/wiki/Branford,_Connecticut

First Congregational Church United Church of Christ, Branford, Connecticut. www.firstcongregationalbranford.org.

James Blacksone Memorial Library. www.blackstone.lioninc.org

"The Story of Nellie Green." Nellie Green's Restaurant. www.nelliegreens.com/legend.html

"Thimble Islands." Wikipedia. http://en.wkipedia.org/wiki/Thimble_Islands

Bridgeport

The Barnum Museum. http://barnum-museum.org

"Bridgeport, Connecticut." Wikipedia. http://en.wikipedia.org/wiki/Bridgeport,_Connecticut

Palmquist, David W. *Bridgeport: A Pictorial History.* Norfolk, VA: Donning Co., 1985.

Clinton

"About the Morgan School." Clinton Public Schools. www.clintonpublic.org/morganhp.htm

"Abraham Pierson." Wikipedia. http://en.wikipedia.org/wiki/Abraham_Pierson

Adler, Peggy. "The Birth of Yale University." Clinton, Connecticut. www.clintonct.org/yale.htm

"Buell, Abel." *Dictionary of American Biography.* vol. III. New York: Charles Scribner's Sons, 1929.

"Eliot, Jared." *Dictionary of American Biography.* vol. VI. New York: Charles Scribner's Sons, 1931.

First Church of Christ Congregational, Clinton, Connecticut. www.firstchurchclinton
.org/about/history.html

"Morgan, Charles." *Dictionary of American Biography.* vol. XIII. New York: Charles Scribner's
Sons, 1934.

Pierce, Henry H. *Colonial Killingworth: A History of Clinton and Killingworth.* Clinton, CT:
Clinton Historical Society, 1976.

"Pond's Creams." Wikipedia. http://en.wikipedia.org/wiki/Pond%27s_Creams

Coastal Fishing and Shellfishing

Funkhouser, David. "Sound Cleaner, Fisheries Shaky." *Hartford Courant,* March 9, 2008.

Save the Sound. "The Long Island Sound Fishery: Flourishing or Floundering?"
Brochure for 18th Annual Long Island Sound Citizens Summit, March 8, 2008,
Bridgeport, CT.

Coastal Weather

Caplovich, Judd. *Blizzard! The Great Storm of '88.* Vernon, CT: VeRo Publishing, 1987.

Connecticut Courant, October 4, 1815.

"Destructive Gale." *Connecticut Journal,* October 2, 1815.

"The Great New England Hurricane of 1938." http://erh.noaa.gov/box/hurricane1938
.htm

"Hurricane of 1938." www.geociies.com/hurricanene/hurr1938.htm

"Killer Snowstorms Leaves [sic] New England Drained." www.mayflowerfamilies.com/
enquirer/weather.htm

"New England Hurricane of 1938." Wikipedia. http://en.wikipedia.org/wiki/
New_England_Hurricane_of_1938.

Tannehill, I. R. "Hurricane of September 16 to 22, 1938." *Monthly Weather Review* 66, no. 9
(September 1938).

Winthrop, John, to Cotton Mather. New London, Connecticut, 12 September 1717.
Massachusetts Historical Society Collections, vol. V and vol. VII, 1793. http://
capecodhistory.us/19th/MHS1793.html

Darien

Case, Henry Jay, and Simon W. Cooper. *Town of Darien, Founded 1641, Incorporated 1820.* Darien, CT: Darien Community Association, 1935.

Castell, Marian. "Mathers of Darien: A History. March 2001." Darien Historical Society. http://historical.darien.org/matherhistory.htm

Connecticut Department of Veterans Affairs. "History of Connecticut Veterans' Home." www.ct.gov/ctva/cwp/view.asp?A=2005&Q=290842

Darien, Connecticut. www.darienct.gov/about_darien/history.htm

"Darien, Connecticut." Wikipedia. http://en.wikipedia.org/wiki/Darien,_Connecticut

"Fitch Home for Soldiers, Noroton Heights." www.rootsweb.ancestry.com/~ctfairfi/pages/darien/card_fitch.html

Liftig, Robert. "Divided Loyalties." *New Canaan, Darien & Rowayton Magazine.* July 2007. www.ncdmag.com

East Haven

"East Haven, Connecticut." Wikipedia. http://en.wikipedia.org/wiki/East_Haven,_Connecticut

Hughes, Sarah E. *History of East Haven.* New Haven: Tuttle, Morehouse & Taylor, 1908.

East Lyme

"Camp Rowland." Global Security. www.globalsecurity.org/military/facility/camp-rowland.htm

Chapman, L. Edgecomb, and Elizabeth Horan Murphy. *Scallop Shells and Granite, Too—East Lyme, Connecticut, 1839–1989.* Mystic, CT: Mystic Publications, 1989.

Connecticut Gazette, June 25, 1790.

"East Lyme, Connecticut." Wikipedia. http://en.wikipedia.org.wiki/East_Lyme,_Connecticut

East Lyme Historical Society. http://eastlymehistoricalsociety.org

"First Regiment Ready for Camp." *Hartford Courant,* July 12, 1913.

"Guardsmen Meet Chilly Weather." *Hartford Courant,* July 16, 1913.

"A Mimic War at Camp Today." *Hartford Courant,* July 18, 1913.

"Troops Are Ready for Sham Battle." *Hartford Courant,* July 17, 1913.

Fairfield

Austen, Barbara E., and Barbara D. Bryan. *Fairfield, Connecticut.* Charleston, SC: Arcadia Publishing, 1997.

Farnham, Thomas J. *Fairfield: The Biography of a Community, 1639–2000.* West Kennebunk, ME: Phoenix Publishing for the Fairfield Historical Society, 2000.

Fairfield Museum and History Center. www.fairfieldhistoricalsociety.org

First Church Congregational United Church of Christ, Fairfield, Connecticut. www .firstchurchfairfield.org

Greenfield Hill Congregational Church. http://greenfieldhillchurch.com/GHCC_ history_page.php

"History of Fairfield—A Summary." Fairfield, Connecticut. www.fairfieldct.org/history .htm

Love, Beth L. *Fairfield and Southport.* Charleston, SC: Arcadia Publishing, 2000.

"The Margaret Rudkin Story." Pepperidge Farm. www.pepperidgefarm.com/ MargaretRudkin.aspx

"Town of Fairfield." www.americantowns.com/ct/fairfield/organization/ town_of_fairfield

Greenwich

Clark, William J. *Greenwich.* Charleston, SC: Arcadia, 2003.

"Clyde Fitch." Wikipedia. http://en.wikipedia.org/wiki/Clyde_Fitch

"Greenwich History." www.rootsweb.ancestry.com/ctfairfi/pages/greenwich/ greenwich_hstry.htm

Historic Putnam Cottage. www.putnamcottage.org/history.html

Historical Society of the Town of Greenwich. http://hstg.org

"History of Greenwich, Connecticut." Wikipedia. http://en.wkipedia.org/wiki/ History_of_Greenwich%2C_Connecticut

Jacobs, Leonard. "Drama of Discovery." Woodlawn Cemetery Newsletter, Fall 2003. www
.thewoodlawncemetery.org/newsletters/fall2003.html

Munk, Nina. "Greenwich's Outrageous Fortunes." *Vanity Fair.* July 2006.

"Viola Allen." Wikipedia. http://en.wikipedia.org/wiki/Viola_Allen

Groton

Andrews, Gregory E., and Karen P. Will. *Town of Groton, Connecticut, Historic Preservation Plan.* August 1996.

Bakowski, Karen. "The History of Morton Plant and Branford House." University of Connecticut Avery Point Campus, Groton, Connecticut. www.branford.uconn .edu/history.htm

"Electric Boat Corporation's History." General Dynamics Electric Boat. www.gdeb.com/ about.history/

Kimball, Carol W., James L. Streeter, and Marilyn J. Comrie. *Groton.* Charleston, SC: Arcadia Publishing, 2004.

"Naval Submarine Base New London." Wikipedia. http://en.wikipedia.org/wiki/ Naval_Submarine_Base_New_London.

Naval Sub Base New London. www.cnic.navy.mil/newlondon/index.htm.

Reyburn, James S. *Electric Boat Corporation.* Charleston, SC: Arcadia Publishing, 2006.

Smith, Carolyn, and Helen Vergason. *September 6, 1781: North Groton's Story.* New London, CT: New London Printers, 1981.

Underhill, John. *Newes From America; Or, a New and Expermentall Discoverie of New England.* London: J.D. for Peter Cole, 1638.

USS *Lafayette* SSBN 616. http://ssbn616.homestead.com/History.html

Guilford

"Aerial Photography in Community Debates on Land Use." Yale University. http:// classes.yale.edu/00-01/amst401a/guilford/wholedoc.html

Bloomer, Nona. *The Guilford Green.* Guilford, CT: Guilford Free Library, 1996.

Clark, Tim. "Guilford, Connecticut." *Yankee Magazine,* May 1989.

Cody, Michael. "Fitz-Greene Halleck." *Dictionary of Literary Biography*, vol. 250. Detroit: Thomson Gale, 2001.

Connecticut Commission on Culture and Tourism. Henry Whitfield State Museum, Guilford, Connecticut. http://whitfieldmuseum.org/

"Fitz-Greene Halleck." Wikipedia. http://en.wikipedia.org/wiki/Fitz-Greene_Halleck

"Guilford Green." Connecticut Trust for Historic Preservation. www.towngreens.com

Guilford Keeping Society. *Guilford.* Charleston, SC: Arcadia Publishing, 2001.

Guilford Preservation Alliance. www.guilfordpreservation.org

Halleck, Fitz-Greene. "Connecticut." *Yale Book of American Verse,* edited by Thomas R. Lounsbury. New Haven: Yale University Press, 1912. www.bartleby.com/102/13.html

Lindsay, James. *Pictorial Guilford: A New England Town in Photographs.* Guilford, CT: Guilford Keeping Society, 1976.

McCulloch, Sarah Brown. *Guilford: A Walking Guide, the Green & Neighboring Streets.* Guilford, CT: Guilford Preservation Society, 1989.

Sexton, James. *The Guilford Green: An Ever-Changing Landscape,* typescript. Hamden, CT: Connecticut Trust for Historic Preservation, 2002.

Steiner, Bernard. *A History of the Plantation of Menunkatuck and of the Original Town of Guilford, Connecticut, Comprising the Present Towns of Guilford and Madison.* Guilford, CT: 1897.

Madison

Cleaver, Merritt W. *The History of North Madison, Connecticut.* rev. ed. Guilford, CT: 2006.

Connecticut Journal, May 23, 1782.

"Cutter Eagle." United States Coast Guard. www.uscg.mil/history/WEBCUTTERS/Eagle_1809.html

"A History of Hammonassett." Friends of Hammonassett. www.friendsofhammonassett.org/history.htm

Lord, Warner P., and Beverly J. Montgomery. *Madison Connecticut in the Twentieth Century.* Dover, NH: Arcadia Publishing, 1998.

Madison Bicentennial Committee. *Madison: Three Hundred Years by the Sea.* Madison, CT: The Committee, 1976.

Madison Historical Society. www.madisoncthistorical.org.

Oedel, Howard T., ed. *Daniel Hand of Madison, Connecticut, 1801–1891*. Madison, CT: Madison Historical Society, 1973.

Platt, Philip S., ed. *Madison's Heritage*. Madison, CT: Madison Historical Society, 1964.

Steiner, Bernard Christian. *A History of the Plantation of Menunkatuck and of the Original Town of Guilford, Connecticut, Comprising the Present Towns of Guilford and Madison*. Guilford: 1897.

Talcott, Alvan, comp. *Families of Early Guilford, Connecticut*. Baltimore: Genealogical Publishing Co., 1984.

Milford

Abbott, Susan Woodruff, comp. *Families of Early Milford, Connecticut*. Baltimore: Genealogical Publishing Company, 1979.

"BIC Corporation—Company History." www.fundinguniverse.com/company-histories/BIC-Corporation-Company-History

First United Church of Christ Congregational, Milford, Connecticut. www.firstchurchofmilford.org

Ford, George Hare. *Historical Sketches of the Town of Milford*. New Haven, CT: Tuttle, Morehouse, and Taylor, 1914.

Greene, M. Louise. "Early Milford." *Connecticut Magazine,* vol. 5, no. 3, March 1899.

Hurd, Melville. *Milford*. Charleston, SC: Arcadia Publishing, 2006.

"Jonathan Law." Connecticut State Library. www.cslib.org/gov/lawj.htm

Milford, Connecticut. www.ci.milford.ct.us

"Milford, Connecticut." Wikipedia. www.reference.com/browse/wiki/Milford,_Connecticut

Milford Historical Society. http://mywebpage.netscape.com/milfordhistoric

"Our History." BIC. www.bicworld.com/inter_us/corporate/history/time_line.asp

Platt, Omar W. *History of Milford, Connecticut, 1639–1939*. Bridgeport, CT: Braunworth & Co., 1939.

"Robert Treat." Connecticut State Library. http://cslib.org/gov/treatr.htm

"Robert Treat." www.rootsweb.com/~genepool/treatrob.htm

St. Gabriel Church, Milford, Connecticut. http://www.stgabchurch.4lpi.com/

"The Schick Story." www.shaving.com/history.asp

"Wilkinson Sword." Wikipedia. http://en.wikipedia.org/wiki/Wilkinson_Sword

A Motley Group of Lighthouses

Claflin, James. *Lighthouses and Life Saving Along the Connecticut and Rhode Island Coast.* Charleston, SC: Arcadia Publishing, 2001.

D'Entremont, Jeremy. *The Lighthouses of Connecticut.* Lighthouse Treasury. Beverly, MA: Commonwealth Editions, 2005.

Lighthousefriends.com

National Park Serivce. "Inventory of Historic Light Stations, Connecticut Lighthouses." www.nps.gov/history/maritime/light/ct.htm

New England Lighthouses. http://lighthouse.cc/menu.html

New Haven

Caplan, Colin M. *New Haven.* Charleston, SC: Arcadia Publishing, 2006.

Foote, George, and Richard Silocka. "New Haven—Maritime History and Arts." Yale-New Haven Teacher's Institute. www.yale.edu/ynhti/curriculum/units/1979/3/79.03.02.x.html

The Grove Street Cemetery. www.grovestreetcemetery.org

"International Festival of Arts & Ideas." Wikipedia. www.artidea.org/view_page.php?id=40

Leeney, Robert. *Elms, Arms & Ivy: New Haven in the Twentieth Century.* Montgomery, AL: Community Communications in cooperation with the New Haven Colony Historical Society, 2000.

"New Haven, Connecticut." Wikipedia. http://en.wikipedia.org/wiki/New_Haven,_Connecticut

Osterweis, Rollin G. *The New Haven Green and the American Bicentennial.* Hamden, CT: Archon Books, 1976.

"Powder House Day." Wikipedia. http://en.wikipedia.org/wiki/Powder_House_Day

"Shubert Theatre (New Haven)." Wikipedia. http://en.wikipedia.org/wiki/Shubert_Theatre_%28New_Haven%29

New London

Caulkins, Frances Manwaring. *History of New London, Connecticut.* New London, CT: H. D. Utley, 1895.

Decker, Robert Owen. *The Whaling City: A History of New London.* Chester, CT: Pequot Press for the New London County Historical Society, 1976.

"Historic Sites of New London, Connecticut." *New London Gazette.* http:// newlondongazette.com/histrc.html

"New London, Connecticut." Wikipedia. http://en.wikipedia.org/wiki/ New_London,_Connecticut.

New London County Historical Society. www.newlondonhistory.org

"The O'Neill Monte Cristo Cottage." Eugene O'Neill Theater Center. www .oneilltheatercenter.org

"Touring Eugene O'Neill's New London." EOneill.com. www.eOneill.com/library/ touring/10.htm

"United States Coast Guard Academy." Wikipedia. http://en.wikipedia.org/wiki/ United_States_Coast_Guard_Academy

Norwalk

"A Brief History of the Maritime Aquarium." The Maritime Aquarium. http:// maritimeaquarium.org/about_history.html.

"Classic Hat Makers List." The Fedora Lounge. www.thefedoralounge.com.

"The History of St. Paul's." St. Paul's on the Green, Norwalk, Connecticut. http:// stpaulsnorwalk.org/history.html.

Lobozza, Carl. *Norwalk, Connecticut: "Pictures from the Past."* Norwalk, CT: Norwalk Historical Society, 1974.

Norwalk, Connecticut. www.norwalkct.org.

"Norwalk, Connecticut." Wikipedia. http://en.wikipedia.org/wiki/ Norwalk_Connecticut.

Norwalk Historical Society. www.norwalkhistoricalsociety.org.

"Norwalk Oyster Festival History." Norwalk Seaport Association. www.seaport.org/ history.htm.

Ray, Deborah Wing, and Gloria P. Stewart. *Norwalk: Being an Historical Account of that Connecticut Town.* Canaan, NH: Phoenix Publishing for the Norwalk Historical Society, 1979.

"The Rise of Organized Labor in Nineteenth Century Connecticut Case Study." Yale-New Haven Teacher's Institute. www.yale.edu/ynhti/curriculum/units/1981/cthistory/81.ch.05.x.html

Old Lyme

"American Impressionism." Wikipedia. http://en.wikipedia.org/wiki/American_Impressionism

Barker, G. Stuart. *Landmarks of Old Lyme, Connecticut.* Old Lyme, CT: Ladies' Library Association of Old Lyme, 1968.

Burton, Kathryn. *Old Lyme, Lyme, and Hadlyme.* Charleston, SC: Arcadia Publishing, 2005.

Crosby, Becky. "A Brief History of the 1st Congregational Church of Old Lyme." The First Congregational Church of Old Lyme, CT. www.besobold.net/~fccol/about/church_history.htm

Devlin, John C., and Grace Naismith. *The World of Roger Tory Peterson: An Authorized Biography.* N.p.: Optimum Publishing Co., 1977.

Ely, Susan Hollingsworth, and Elizabeth B. Plimpton. *The Lieutenant River.* Lyme's Heritage Series. Old Lyme, CT: Lyme Historical Society and Florence Griswold Museum, 1991.

Florence Griswold Museum, Old Lyme, Connecticut. www.flogris.org

"Impressionism." Wikipedia. http://en.wikipedia.org/wiki/Impressionism

Martin, Douglas. "Elizabeth Tashjian, 94, an Expert on Nuts, Dies." *New York Times,* February 4, 2007.

"Matthew Griswold: Governor of Connecticut, 1784–1786." Connecticut State Library. www.cslib.org/gov/griswoldm.htm

"The Nut Museum: Visionary Art of Elizabeth Tashjian." www.tfaoi.com/aa/4aa/4aa291.htm

Old Lyme, Connecticut. www.oldlyme-ct.gov

Old Lyme Historic District Commission. *Old Lyme Historic District Handbook.* Old Lyme, CT: Historic District Commission, 2001.

"Peterson, Roger Tory." American National Biography Online. www.anb.org/
articles/13/13-02617-article.html

State of Connecticut. Office of the Governor. "Roger Tory Peterson Wildlife Area in Old
Lyme Dedicated." www.ct.gov/governorrell/cwp/view.asp?A=11&Q=257534

Stevens, Thomas A. *Old Lyme: A Town Inexorably Linked with the Sea.* Essex, CT: Connecticut
River Foundation, 1959.

Woodside, Christine. "The Nut Lady Believed It Was Art. Now, a College Agrees." *New
York Times,* August 4, 2002.

Old Saybrook

"Fenwick, Connecticut." Wikipedia. http://en.wikipedia.org/wiki/
Fenwick,_Connecticut

Grant, Ellsworth. "The Main Stream of New England." *American Heritage,* April 1967.

Lucas, Beverly. "Fenwick-on-the-Sound from Public Playground to Private Borough."
Review of Exhibition at the Connecticut River Museum at Steamboat Dock,
Essex, CT. *Connecticut History* 43, no. 1 (spring 2004): 174–78.

Old Saybrook, Connecticut. www.oldsaybrookct.org

Recreation

Reynolds, Edith. *Savin Rock Amusement Park.* Postcard History Series. Charleston, SC:
Arcadia Publishing, 2006.

Savin Rock Museum. www.savinrockmuseum.com

Stamford

"The Badge of Military Merit." Connecticut Society Sons of the American Revolution.
www.connecticutsar.org/articles/badge_of_military_merit.htm

Baulsir, Linda, and Irwin Miller. *The Jewish Communities of Greater Stamford.* Charleston, SC:
Arcadia Publishing, 2002.

"Charles Henry Phillips." Wikipedia. http://en.wikipedia.org/wiki/Charles_Henry_
Phillips

"Clairol to close Stamford plant by 2010." *Stamford Advocate,* June 8, 2007. www.tmcnet
.com/usubmit/2007/06/08/2699800.htm

"Col. Jacob Schick." http://iavbbs.com/gflinn/schick.htm

Feinstein, Estelle F. "Stamford, Connecticut, 1641–1893: The first two-and-a-half
centuries." Stamford Historical Society. www.stamfordhistory.org/feinhist.htm

———. *Stamford from Puritan to Patriot: The Shaping of a Connecticut Community, 1641–
1774.* Stamford, CT: Stamford Bicentennial Corporation, 1976.

———. *Stamford in the Gilded Age: The Political Life of a Connecticut Town, 1868–1893.*
Stamford, CT: Stamford Historical Society, 1973.

Gershon, Eric. "Royal Bank of Scotland Building Rises in Stamford." *Hartford Courant,*
April 22, 2008.

"History of Stamford, Connecticut." www.answers.com/topic/history-of-stamford-
connecticut?cat=travel

"The history of Yale locks." Yale Lock Company. www.yalelock.com

"Linus Yale, Jr." Wikipedia. http://en.wikipedia.org/wiki/Linus_Yale,_Jr

"Long Island's Loyalists: The Misunderstood Americans." OBHS Freeholder Magazine
Online. http://members.aol.com/obhistory/freeab.htm

Loyalist Collection of the University of Brunswick. www.lib.unb.ca/collections/loyalist

Loyalist Trails UELAC Newsletter, online edition, 2007 archive. United Empire Loyalists'
Association of Canada. www.uelac.org/Loyalist-Trails/2007/
Loyalist-Trails-2007.php?issue=200745

Loyalist Trails UELAC Newsletter, online edition, 2007 archive. United Empire Loyalists'
Association of Canada. www.uelac.org/Loyalist-Trails/2007/
Loyalist-Trails-2007.php?issue=200732

"Padlock." Wikipedia. http://en.wikipedia.org/wiki/Padlock

"Pin tumbler lock." Wikipedia. http://en.wikipedia.org/wiki/Pin_tumbler_lock

Stamford Historical Society. www.stamfordhistory.org

Stamford Historical Society. www.cslib.org/stamford/

Stonington

Mystic Aquarium & Institute for Exploration. www.mysticaquarium.org

Mystic River Historical Society. *Mystic.* Charleston, SC: Arcadia Publishing, 2004.

Palmer, Henry Robinson. *Stonington by the Sea*. 2nd ed. Stonington, CT: Palmer Press, 1957.

Stonington Borough, Connecticut. www.stoningtonboroughct.com.

Stonington Historical Society. www.stoningtonhistory.org.

Stratford

Calhoun, John D., and Lewis G. Knapp. *Stratford*. Charleston, SC: Arcadia Publishing, 2004.

Christ Episcopal Church, Stratford, Connecticut. www.christchurchstratford.org/history

"Igor I. Sikorsky." Igor I. Sikorsky Historical Archives, Inc. www.sikorskyarchives.com/siksky2.html

"Igor Sikorsky—VS-300." U.S. Centennial of Flight Commission. www.centennialofflight.gov/essay/Rotary/Sikorsky_VS300/HE8.htm

"Johnson, William Samuel." Biographical Directory of the United States Congress. http://bioguide.congress.gov/scripts/biodisplay.pl?index=J000182

Knapp, Lewis G. *Stratford and the Sea*. Charleston, SC: Arcadia Publishing, 2002.

"Stratford, Connecticut." Wikipedia. http://en.wikipedia.org/wiki/Stratford,_Connecticut

Stratford, Connecticut. www.townofstratford.com.

Wilcoxson, William Howard. *History of Stratford, Connecticut, 1639–1939*. Stratford, CT: Stratford Tercentenary Commission, 1939.

Traveling Up and Down the Coast

"Merritt Parkway." Wikipedia. http://en.wikipedia.org/wiki/Merritt_Parkway

"Merritt Parkway Conservancy." www.merittparkway.org

The Shore Line Trolley Museum. www.bera.org.

Turner, Gregg M., and Melancthon W. Jacobus. *Connecticut Railroads: An Illustrated History*. Hartford: The Connecticut Historical Society, 1986.

Waterford

Bachman, Robert L. *An Illustrated History of the Town of Waterford*. Waterford, CT: Bicentennial Committee, Town of Waterford, 2000.

Caulkins, Frances Manwaring. *History of New London, Connecticut.* New London, CT: H. D. Utley, 1895.

Connecticut Department of Environmental Protection. Fort Trumbull State Park. www.ct.gov/dep/cwp/view.asp?A=2716&Q=325200

———. Harkness Memorial State Park. www.ct.gov/dep/cwp/view.asp?a=2716&q=325214&depNav_GID=1650

Connecticut Humanities Council. "Quakers, Shakers, and Rogerenes." Laptop Encyclopedia of Connecticut History. www.ctheritage.org/biography/topical_religion/quakers.htm

Duchesneau, John. "The History of Fort Trumbull." www.geocities.com/~jmgould/trumhist.html

Grant, Steve. "A Religious Movement You've Never Heard Of." *Hartford Courant,* August 4, 2002.

Greene, M. Louise. *The Development of Religious Liberty in Connecticut.* Boston: Moughton, Mifflin, and Company, 1905.

"Millstone Nuclear Power Plant." Wikipedia. http://en.wikipedia.org/wiki/Millstone_Nuclear_Power_Plant

Pawlowski, John A. *Connecticut Mining.* Charleston, SC: Arcadia Publishing, 2006.

Reed, Willard A., III. *The Granite Industry of Waterford.* Waterford, CT: 1997.

"Rogerenes." Adherents.com: National & World Religion Statistics—Church Statistics—World Religions. www.adherents.com/adhloc/Wh_79.html

"The Rogerenes," in *Strange Stories, Amazing Facts of America's Past.* N.p: Reader's Digest Association, 1989. www.rogersgenealogy.com/downloads/Rogerenes/readersdigest.htm

Westbrook

"Esther Lape." Eleanor Roosevelt National Historic Site, Hyde Park, New York. www.nps.gov/archive/elro/glossary/lape-esther.htm

First Congregational Church, United Church of Christ, Westbrook, Connecticut. www.westcongchurch.org

First Congregational Church of Westbrook. *A Church History on Our 250th Anniversary, 1726–1976.* N.p., 1976.

Potapaug Audubon Society. www.potapaugaudubon.org/nature_center/

Roosevelt, Eleanor. "My Day, September 22, 1945." www.gwu.edu/~erpapers/myday/
displaydoc.cfm?_y=1945_f=md000137

"Submarine Technology Through the Years." Chief of Naval Operations, Submarine
Warfare Division. www.navy.mil/navydata/cno/n87/history/subhistory.html.

West Haven

North, Harriet C., and Bennett W. Dorman. "A Brief History of West Haven . . . written
in 1986." Savin Rock Museum. http://savinrockmuseum.com/whhistory.htm

West Haven Historical Society. *West Haven.* Charleston, SC: Arcadia Publishing, 2005.

Westport

"Compo House. The Residence of Richard H. Winslow Esq. at Westport, Conn." George
Glazer Gallery, New York. www.georgeglazer.com/prints/aanda/historic/
compo.html

The Congregational Church of Green's Farms. www.greensfarmschurch.org/history.htm

"Forty People Who Made a Difference." *Westport Magazine,* January 2007. www
.westportmag.com/media/Westport-Magazine/January-2007/40-People-Who-
Made-a-Difference

Foster, Joanna. *Stories from Westport's Past.* Westport, CT: 1985.

"John Davis Lodge." Wikipedia. http://en.wikipedia.org.wiki/John_Davis_Lodge

Westport, Connecticut. www.westportct.gov

"Westport, Connecticut." Wikipedia. http://en.wikipedia.org/wiki/
Westport,_Connecticut

Westport Country Playhouse. www.westportplayhouse.org

PHOTO CREDITS

All illustrations are from the collections of The Connecticut Historical Society.

Riverside Rowing Club: Photograph. See p. 174. Connecticut coastline, 1813, DETAIL of Connecticut, from the best authorities: Engraved map by Amos Doolittle. Connecticut coastline, 1875, DETAIL of New Map of Connecticut: Lithographic map by Samuel D. Tilden. p. 2 Genl. Israel Putnam: Lithograph by E.B. & E.C. Kellogg. p. 3 Horse Show Day at Belle Haven: Postcard. p. 4-5 Fitch and Allen: Photograph. p. 6-7 View of Long Island Sound: Photograph. p. 8 Pickwick Arms Hotel: Postcard. p. 11 Broadside for Yale & Towne Manufacturing Co. p. 12-13 SW view of Stamford: Drawing by John Warner Barber. p. 14 Congregation Agudath Sholom: Postcard. p. 16-17 Stamford, Conn.: Lithograph by Beck & Pauli. p. 18 Stamford: Photograph by Robert J. Bitondi. p. 21 Fitch's Home, Noroton Heights. Postcard, ca. 1910. p. 22-23 SW view of the Congregational Church, Darien: Drawing by John Warner Barber. p. 24 Congregational Church, Darien: Postcard. p. 26 Club House at Tokeneke Beach: Postcard. p. 28 Loyalist officer's uniform coat, Gift of Henry L. Mills. p. 29 Redware plate, The Newman S. Hungerford Museum Fund. p. 30-31 E. view of Old Well: Drawing by John Warner Barber. p. 32-33 S. view of Norwalk: Drawing by John Warner Barber. p. 36-37 East Beach, Bell Is.: Photograph. p. 38-39 Spectators at bicycle race: Photograph. p. 42 Minute Man statue: Postcard. p. 43 Exhibition of fireworks: Broadside. p. 44-45 View in the central part of Westport: Drawing by John Warner Barber. p. 46-47 S. view of Saugatuck Bridge and village: Drawing by John Warner Barber. p. 46 Atwell and Tolley: Photograph. p. 50 Steamer City of Hartford: Lithograph by Charles R. Parsons. The Newman S. Hungerford Museum Fund. p. 51 New Haven and Northampton Canal Boat Line: Broadside. p. 52 New York and New Haven steamboat line: Broadside. p. 53 Turnpike Tickets: Engravings by Amos Doolittle. p. 53 Pequot Wheel Club: Photograph. p. 54-55 Horse-drawn omnibus: Photograph. p. 56 Hartford and New Haven Railroad: Broadside. p. 57 Pope Company outing: Photograph. p. 58 Bridge on the Merritt Parkway: Photograph. p. 60 Burning of Fairfield: Wood-engraved book illustration from Goodrich, *History of CT.* p. 61 W. view of the Buckley tavern: Drawing by John Warner Barber. p. 62-63 E. view of the Court House, church, and jail: Drawing by John Warner Barber. p. 64-65 N. view of the Academy and church on Greenfield Hill: Drawing by John Warner Barber. p. 66 Pulpit on the Rock: Postcard. p. 67 Boyle's Beach Casino: Photograph. p. 68 Cottages along the shore: Postcard. p. 71 Bridgeport: Drawing by John Warner Barber. p. 72 Iranistan: Wood-engraving. p. 73 A. L. Cheney & Co.: Photograph. p. 74-75 Bridgeport, Conn., 1882: Lithograph by Charles Hart and W.O. Laughna Art Publishing Co. p. 76 Circus in Winter Quarters: Detail of Bridgeport, Conn., 1882. p. 76 Baseball: Bridgeports vs. New Britains: Broadside. p. 77 Broadside for the Locomobile Company of America. p. 78 Bridgeport Brass parade float: Photograph. p. 79 Aerial view of Bridgeport Harbor: Photograph by Publishers Photo Service. p. 83 William Samuel Johnson: Engraving. p. 84 SW view of the Church and the Academy at Stratford: Drawing by John Warner Barber. p. 85 Along the Housatonic: Watercolor. p. 86 Robert Brandt: Photograph by David French. p. 87 Igor Sikorsky and helicopter: Photograph. p. 90 Stowe House: Photograph. p. 91 S. view of the Churches in Milford: Drawing by John Warner Barber. p. 92 Memorial Bridge: Photograph. p. 93-4 Broad Street, Milford: Postcard. p. 98 St. Gabriel's R.C. Church: Postcard. p. 101 The Green, West Haven: Postcard. p. 102 West Haven Ladies' Seminary: Broadside. p. 103 Flying Horses: Broadside. p. 104 Pebble of Oyster River: Postcard. p. 107 Beach at Westbrook: Photograph by R.S. DeLamater. p. 107 Steele and Annis family: Photograph. p. 108 Hammonasset Beach: Postcard. p. 108 The Ark, Indian Neck: Postcard. p. 109 Sachem's Head Hotel: Brochure with wood-engravings by John William Orr. p. 109 Montowese House: Postcard. p. 110 Griswold Inn: Photograph. p. 110 Cottages at White Beach: Photograph. p. 111 Sleepy Hollow Cabins: Postcard, Gift of

Penny Wood. p. 112 The Midway, Savin Rock: Postcard. p. 112 The Devil, Savin Rock: Postcard. p. 113 Chute the Chutes, Savin Rock: Postcard. p. 113 Mr. and Mrs. Marshall Brown and friends: Tintype. p. 114 Circus parade, New Haven: Photograph. p. 114 Sailboat at Mulberry Point: Postcard. p. 115 Men's outing: Photograph. p. 115 The Midway, Roton Point: Postcard. p. 117 Plan of the Town of New Haven: Engraving. p. 118 Yale College: Wood-engraving by John Warner Barber. p. 120-21 E. View of the Green in New Haven: Wood-engraving by John Warner Barber. p. 122 Yale College and state house: Lithograph by D.W. Kellogg & Co. p. 123 Cinque: Mezzotint by John Sartain. p. 124 Female operatives patching and packing bullets: Wood-engraving from *Frank Leslie's Illustrated Newspaper.* p. 125 City of New Haven: Lithograph by O.H. Bailey & Co. p. 126 Boys running beside horse-drawn fire wagon: Photograph. p. 127 Sulla and Starano wedding party: Photograph. p. 128 C. S. Mersick and Company: Photograph. p. 132 NW view of the churches, East Haven: Drawing by John Warner Barber. p. 133 S. part of Saltonstalls pond: Drawing by John Warner Barber. p. 134-35 Foxon Road: Photograph. p. 136 Connecticut Company outing, sack race, broad jump: Photographs. p. 137 Congregational Church: Photograph. p. 140 W. view of the churches and Academy in Branford: Drawing by John Warner Barber. p. 141 Sam's first store: Photograph. p. 142 Workmen with stone for Bulkeley Bridge: Photograph. p. 142 Thimble Islands: Postcard. p. 143 Bird's Eye View of Branford: Lithograph by Hughes & Bailey. p. 144 Ella Wheeler Wilcox: Frontispiece from *An Erring Woman's Love.* p. 145 The 'Bungalow,' (Ella Wheeler Wilcox House): Postcard. p. 146 Farm River Motor Boat Club (later Nellie Green House): Postcard. p. 150 SW view of the ancient Stone House: Drawing by John Warner Barber. p. 151 Henry Whitfield House: Photograph by John Frederick Kelly. p. 152 View of Guilford: Lithograph by O.H. Bailey & Co. p. 153 I. S. Spencer's Sons Iron Founders: Photograph. p. 154-55 Guilford green: Detail of lithograph by O.H. Bailey & Co. p. 156 Rustic Inn: Postcard. p. 157 Grass Island: Photograph by Bo Kass. p. 159 Captain Phineas Meigs's hat. Gift of Colonel Phineas Meigs. p. 160 Lee's Academy and Congregational Church: Drawing by John Warner Barber. p. 161 Hand Academy: Postcard. p. 162 Boston Post Road, Madison: Postcard. p. 163 Short-term camps, Hammonasset: Postcard. p. 166 New London Harbor Lighthouse: Photograph. p. 167 Bridgeport Lighthouse: Photograph. p. 168 New London Ledge Lighthouse: Postcard. p. 170-71 Killingworth: Drawing by John Warner Barber. p. 172 Carter's Inn tavern sign. Collection of Morgan B. Brainard, Gift of Maxwell L. Brainard. p. 173 Vegetable soap: Broadside. p. 174-75 Morgan School: Detail of Lithograph by O.H. Bailey & Co. p. 176-77 View of Clinton: Lithograph by O.H. Bailey & Co. p. 180 Northwest view of Westbrook: Drawing by John Warner Barber. p. 181 Old Kirtland homestead: Photograph. p. 182 Westbrook: Photograph by R.S. DeLamater. p. 184 Cottages: Photograph by R.S. DeLamater. p. 185 Happy Fourth of July: Photograph. p. 188 Lady Fenwick's Monument: Drawing by John Warner Barber. p. 189 James Pharmacy: Photograph. p. 190 Fenwick Hall: Photograph. p. 191 Leverett Brainard cottage: Photograph. p. 192 Aetna Outing, Fenwick Hall: Photograph. p. 194 Riverside Rowing Club: Photograph. p. 197 W. view of Lyme: Drawing by John Warner Barber. p. 198 S. view of Gov. Griswold's House: Drawing by John Warner Barber. p. 199 Shopping scene at Sound View: Postcard. p. 200 Church at Old Lyme: Etching by Childe Hassam. p. 202 Florence Griswold in her dining room: Postcard. p. 206 Bride Brook wedding float: Photograph by G.R. Anderson. p. 207 Thomas Lee House: Postcard. p. 208 Ye Church at East Lyme: Drawing. p. 209 Sham battle, Connecticut National Guard: Photograph. p. 210 2d Reg. Doing 'Tango': Photograph. p. 212 Snow tunnel, Bridgeport: Photograph. p. 213 Clearing train tracks, South Norwalk: Photograph. p. 213 Cannon Street, Bridgeport: Photograph by Charles R. Bronson. p. 214 Hurricane of 1938: Grove Beach: Photograph. p. 215 Hurricane of 1938: Hawk's Nest: Photograph. p. 215 Hurricane of 1938; Tulip on shore: Photograph. p. 216 Hurricane of 1938: train off tracks, Stonington: Photograph. p. 219 Fort Trumbull: Postcard. p. 221 Shanties at Millstone: Photograph. p. 222-23 Maypole at Sandy Point: Photograph. p. 227 Hempsted House: Postcard. p. 228 Shaw Mansion: Postcard. p. 229 American Whaler: Lithograph by E.C. Kellogg. p. 230-31 Whale Oil Row:

ABOUT THE AUTHOR

Diana Ross McCain is a historian who has written about Connecticut's past for more than twenty-five years. She holds bachelor's and master's degrees in history and has been a frequent contributor to *Early American Life* and *Connecticut* magazines, and to the *Hartford Courant*. She wrote the award-winning publication *To All on Equal Terms*, the story of Connecticut's official state heroine, Prudence Crandall. She is the author of *It Happened in Connecticut*, also published by the Globe Pequot Press. McCain was also on the staff of the Connecticut Historical Society, first as a librarian, then as public information officer, for twenty years. She lives in Durham, Connecticut.

ABOUT CHS

The Connecticut Historical Society is a nonprofit museum, library, and education center, located in Hartford, Connecticut. Its mission is to inspire and foster a lifelong interest in history through exhibitions, programs, and Connecticut-related collections, because examining and understanding the past, and connecting the past with the present, provide a guide for the future.

Established in Hartford in 1825, CHS is one of the oldest historical societies in the nation and houses one of the most distinguished museum and library collections in New England. These collections include more than 242,000 prints and photographs and 38,000 objects, with strengths in seventeenth- and eighteenth-century furniture; costume and textiles; portraits and landscapes; tavern and trade signs; decorative arts; toys; tools; more than 125,000 printed books; 1,300 maps; 3,700 broadsides; and three million manuscripts, including one of the nation's finest genealogical collections.

Access to CHS holdings is available through the research center at 1 Elizabeth Street in Hartford, where selections from the collections are also on view in permanent and changing exhibitions designed for adults and families. Public programs and events for adults and families offer a fun way for individuals to think about history and learn from the society's collections. CHS offers a wide range of educational programs for students in grades kindergarten through 12 and is Connecticut's host for National History Day.